BRITISH LABOUR STRUGGLES:
CONTEMPORARY PAMPHLETS 1727-1850

CHARACTER, OBJECT

AND

EFFECTS OF TRADES' UNIONS

1834

[Edward Carleton Tufnell]

Arno Press

A New York Times Company/New York 1972

Reprint Edition 1972 by Arno Press Inc.

Reprinted from copies in the Kress Library
Graduate School of Business Administration,
Harvard University

BRITISH LABOUR STRUGGLES: CONTEMPORARY PAMPHLETS 1727-1850
ISBN for complete set: 0-405-04410-0

See last pages for complete listing.

Manufactured in the United States of America

Library of Congress Cataloging in Publication Data

Tufnell, Edward Carleton.
    Character, object, and effects of trades' unions.

    (British labour struggles:
contemporary pamphlets 1727-1850)
    Reprint of the 1834 ed.
    1. Trade-unions--Great Britain. I. Title.
II. Series.
HD6664.T79 1972   331.88'0942   72-2551
ISBN 0-405-04442-9

CHARACTER, OBJECT,

AND

𝔈ffects

OF

T R A D E S' U N I O N S;

WITH

SOME REMARKS ON THE LAW
CONCERNING THEM.

" The love of freedom is the impulse of an enlightened and presiding spirit, ever intent upon the welfare of the community, or body to which it belongs, and ready to give the alarm, when it beholds any unlawful conspiracy formed, whether it be of rulers or of subjects, with a design to oppress it."—ROBERT HALL.

LONDON:

JAMES RIDGWAY AND SONS, PICCADILLY.

MDCCCXXXIV.

CHARACTER, OBJECT & EFFECTS

OF

Trades' Unions.

Menenius. There was a time, when all the body's members
Rebell'd against the belly; thus accus'd it—
That only like a gulf it did remain
I' the midst o' the body, idle and inactive,
Still cupboarding the viand, never bearing
Like labour with the rest; where the other instruments
Did see, and hear, devise, instruct, walk, feel,
Aud mutually participate, did minister
Unto the appetite and affection common
Of the whole body.
* * * * * * * *

Menenius. For examine
Their counsels, and their cares; digest things rightly,
Touching the weal o' the common; you shall find
No public benefit, which you receive,
But it proceeds, or comes, from them to you,
And no way from yourselves. —CORIOLANUS, Act. I. Scene 1.

THE facts contained in the following account have
been derived from Parliamentary documents, from
a well written pamphlet published two years ago,
entitled "Combinations of Trades," but principally from personal communication with manufacturers, who have seen or suffered the effects of
Combinations. The names of those, who have
supplied the information, have been suppressed,
generally at their own request, as many of them
have stated, and this fact may give some idea of
the terror inspired by these Societies, that their
property and perhaps their lives might be endangered, were it publicly known that they had in-
terested themselves in exposing the character of
Trades' Unions. It is feared that several errors
may have been committed, of which the excuse

B

must be, that they could not easily be avoided by diligence, since the subject relates to Societies bound together by oaths of secrecy.

SECTION I.

The most powerful, extensive, and best organized Union in the kingdom, appears to be that of the working cotton spinners. All, or nearly all the workmen of this class in England, Scotland, and Ireland have been united together in their respective districts for the space of thirty years or more : these district Unions have during that time frequently held communication with each other, but we are not aware that any attempt was made prior to 1829, to form one "grand general Union" of all the spinners of the three kingdoms. Since that time the operations of this combination have been conducted on a more systematic plan ; each town or village, according to the numbers of its spinning population, has elected representatives, who have held *Parliaments*, levied taxes on their constituents, passed laws, printed their speeches and proceedings, and performed all the functions of a legislative body with as much formality as the House of Commons. The institution of this assembly, however, does not appear to have had any marked effect on the trade ; the strikes and other *offensive* business of the Union, were still for the most part decided on by the local committees, and the expense of sending delegates to some central spot, such as the Isle of Man or Manchester, the usual places of meeting, has prevented the holding of a general congress more than once or at most twice a year, and then the Session has not continued longer than four or five days. As the reader may be curious to see how the Spinners' Parliament conducts its business, we give as a specimen one of the discussions at the meeting held at Ramsey, Isle of Man, in 1829. It is necessary to premise, that each member is called by the title of the place he represents, and when more than a single representative is sent from any town, a number accompanies the name to distinguish one from the other. Two real names only are given in the report, one is that of Mr. Doherty the secretary, and the other of Mr. Foster, who appears to have been an interloper, attending the meeting at his own expense, and of whom we are told in the printed account of the proceedings, that " it is but doing him justice to say, that his superior talents contributed very materially to facilitate the business of the meeting."

PRESTON moved, and MANCHESTER seconded.—That one grand general union of all the operative spinners in the United Kingdom be now formed, for the mutual support and protection of all.

GLASGOW wished Mr. Foster or Mr. Doherty to state their views of this very important question, as to how such a union ought to exist, and whether it would be better to have three committees or one only.

Mr. FOSTER said, that in his opinion there should be three committees, one in each kingdom. He was sure that any other plan would not give general satisfaction. Each nation should manage its own affairs, and keep its own money.

JOHNSTONE 1, thought that one head would answer the purpose best. It would hardly be possible to proceed with three different controlling powers. There were a great many objections to three committees, and many circumstances in favour of one.

BOLTON 1, had received instructions from his constituents to oppose one committee to manage all. Each kingdom should manage its own affairs.

MR. DOHERTY said, that three committees might, in the mean time, remove any petty jealousy that might exist as to the precedency, but he was quite satisfied that one head would be much preferable to three. They had come there for the purpose of forming one union and not three. But, according to the plan proposed by Mr. Foster, they would he establishing three.

MR. FOSTER said, that it was very strange that his friend Mr. Doherty should oppose the same thing here, which he advocated at home. According to their union in England, each district had as much control over the affairs of the union as another. No one district could interfere with another. He could not see why one district should be raised up into a head over all the rest.—Mr. Doherty knew that Manchester, in their union in England had no more to do with Bolton, or any other district, nor Bolton with Manchester, than any two separate things.

GLASGOW 2 thought that each district should keep their own money, and the cheques, for security, be distributed through the three kingdoms.

JOHNSTONE would support the opinion of Glasgow as to the money and cheques. Each district should manage its own affairs, without the interference of any other district, but all to contribute to the same general fund.

BOLTON 1 wished to know whether it was intended to give as many cheques to Ireland and Scotland, as to England. If that were so, he thought they would be giving to those places more control over the money than would be consistent with right.—The money should be divided in proportion to the number of payers.

JOHNSTONE 1 was decidedly of opinion that there should be but one grand general Committee. Any other mode of management would but retard their progress. As to the distribution of the money, he concurred with Bolton, that it should be regulated by the number of payers. Suppose, for instance, there are but two districts in Scotland, and perhaps twenty in England, it would not be fair to give as many cheques to Scotland as to England. They would of course, in fairness, be entitled to receive cheques in the proportion of twenty to two.

GLASGOW 1 supported Mr. Foster's views as to the propriety of having three different Committees. He was sure that it would give most satisfaction to their body in Glasgow.

MANCHESTER thought that one general Committee would not give general satisfaction. He feared there would be many objections to it. His own opinion, however was, that if it could be done, it would be preferable to any other mode of management. He would therefore still persist in pressing his motion.

OLDHAM supported the motion.

Mr. FOSTER said, that with regard to what had been said about districts, and the division of the money, he thought it was quite unnecessary. Each nation would be but one district, according to his plan, and each kingdom would have one national Committee. So that if money was wanted by any one district, all they would have to do would be to write a letter to the national Committees, and thus save the trouble and expense of sending out delegates, in cases of emergency, which frequently swallowed up more than the product of all their missions. (Hear! Hear!)

Mr. Doherty. My friend, Mr. Foster, seems to have jumped to a conclusion all at once. He will not endure one district having any more power or control than another. How then is he to form his national Committee ? If such a Committee be formed, it must sit somewhere, and whether it be in Manchester, Bolton, or Oldham, matters nothing. Wherever it be held, that district will have more power than some other districts, for Mr. Foster cannot suppose, that each district either can or will send a person from remote places to attend at each Committee meeting. As that cannot be done, the Committee must be formed in some one district. We are not now enquiring in which district this one general Committee should be formed, but whether such a power should exist. For his own part, he thought that the adoption of national Committees would be attended with much inconvenience. They would suppose that the national Committees, as they had been called, would be formed in Glasgow, Belfast, and Manchester. Then supposing any district had notice of a reduction, if it were Johnstone for instance, they would have to write first to their national Committee at Glasgow. The national Committee would then have to write to the other national Committees at Manchester and Belfast. Then these national Committees must write to all the districts within their respective *territories* requesting to know what Johnstone is to do in their emergency, then the national Committees must wait for an answer from each place, before they can answer the national Committee at Glasgow, and of course, before they can answer the Committee at Johnstone. But by the adoption of one general Committee, a great deal of roundabout writing would be saved. In that case, all that would have to be done, would be for Johnstone, or any other district, to write off at once to the general Committee, or head, and they to each of the districts. Thus, much less time would be lost, in getting the opinion of the whole trade, than by the circuitous rout of national Committees. By the adoption of national Committees, we incur all the evils which Mr. Foster, and those on that side of the question, seem so anxious to avoid, namely, the raising of one district over the others, without securing any of the advantages of having but one head to consult and direct. It was only necessary to extend the principle of the district Union in England, for which Mr. Foster was an advocate, and say, that instead of being confined to England, they should extend to, and embrace every district in the United Kingdom.—They were but one trade, and he could not see why they should attempt to create, or perpetuate distinctions as to nations, while they were all bound by the same laws, injured by the same means, or benefited by the same cause. Their interests were bound up together. And he really could not help expressing his surprise at the course which his friend had taken in the discussion. He was sure that it must appear evident to every man, that one government would answer better than three.

JOHNSTONE thought that one Committee must be adopted. That of course would not interfere with the internal management of the affairs of the several districts. Each district would manage its own local matters, independently of the general Committee. He, as one district, would not like to be too much shackled. If they had a national Committee in Glasgow, for instance, their meetings must be held after eight o'clock at night, when men had finished their day's work. Now, how could he, or any one else from his district, go seventeen miles, after that hour, to attend a meeting, and return again to get any rest, to enable them to follow their work next day? The thing was quite impracticable. It was evident, therefore, that whatever form of government they chose, the Committee composing or forming that government, must be chosen from one district. And he could see no more objection to having one general Committee in England, (or wherever it might be) than having a national Committee in Glasgow. By this plan of national Committees, they would have three Unions instead of one.—And on that ground the plan was objectionable. Whatever way he viewed it, he thought one general head would answer the best end.

MR. FOSTER was sorry that there should be such a diversity of opinions on this plain question. Much had been said that was quite unnecessary. He begged to ask Mr. Doherty, where his one Committee could get its authority? Of whom it was to be composed, and where it was to sit? Mr. Doherty wanted one general Committee, but had not had the boldness to tell them who were to form this all in all! (a laugh.) By the plan he had proposed, they would prevent any one district from arrogating to itself the supreme power, as Mr. Doherty seemed to wish for.—All that the national Committees would do would be to split up the authority into three, instead of having one great superior. He was really much surprised to hear Mr. Doherty advocate one Committee only. He was sure, from the experience he had had on this business, that he should know better than to entertain a hope that they could go on with a system that would give to any one district a controlling power over the rest. Did he forget that he could not form a Union, on that principle, even in England? Does he forget, too, that the last district Union was broken up, principally, if not entirely, on account of its being formed on the same principle which he is now attempting to place this on? The Union which they had lately formed in England would not allow either Mr. Doherty or Manchester to have the ruling power. They had formed a Committee from the various districts. And was it likely that they would suffer Manchester, or Glasgow, or Belfast, or any other place, to assume the power there, at the Isle of Man, which they had already refused them at home. As to the great difficulty which Mr. Doherty had raised, and which he was sorry to hear, had been supported by their friend from Johnstone, it amounted to nothing. All that would be required more, in case of an attempt to reduce either Johnstone, or any where else, would be two letters more than would be necessary by Mr. Doherty's plan—one to each of the other two national Committees. Certainly there should be an executive Committee. But that was all that was necessary. The annual meetings would, of course, make the laws, and they must be made so plain as to need no expounding. The one head that Mr. Doherty seemed so fond of, would be found in the annual meetings. They only should have the power which Mr. Doherty wished to secure in his one Committee. Really, the ambition of Mr. Doherty was equal to his arguments. He was to have one grand Committee to manage the affairs of the whole Union, and he would sit at the foot of the table, (as he then did) as secretary for the three kingdoms! It might, perhaps, be desirable to have such a head as had been alluded to, but he was sure it neither would, nor could, give satisfaction. As to three heads, it might as well be said that there were three kings in England, one for Scotland and one for Ireland, or sixteen heads in the United States of America, as that there would be three heads formed by the formation of three national Committees. He must oppose the for- mation of one Committee.

BOLTON 2 and Mr. Doherty rose at the same time. The latter said that he was aware he had rose out of his turn, but that the extraordinary speech of Mr. Foster called for a reply from him before they proceeded any further. (Cries of hear! hear! hear!) Mr. Foster had done little more than repeat his former arguments. He had talked of three kings, and sixteen heads in the United States of America. Surely he could not be ignorant that the very facts which he adduced, to illustrate his position, formed the strongest arguments against the conclusions. We certainly had three kingdoms, politically speaking, but we had only one king. The King was the head of the three, just as the Committee which he proposed would be the head of the whole Union. According to Mr Foster's plan, he would really have sixteen heads in America, instead of one. Mr. Foster, finding that he could not satisfy his own mind with arguments in favour of his own favourite plan, had had recourse to a most unworthy artifice, with the view of driving him from his position. He endeavoured to make it appear that he was advocating the formation of one Committee, for the mean and shallow gratification of his own vanity. Now few men knew him better than Mr. Foster, and he would put it to him, whether he ever knew him, in any one instance, to support any measure for the purpose of promoting his own interests, or gratifying his vanity?

MR. FOSTER—No! never! (Applause). Then he, Mr. Doherty, thought it most improper to attempt to divert people's attention from the merits of the question, by imputing unworthy motives to his opponents, or to carry the question by throwing out insinuations which he did not believe.—(Hear! hear!) He had said also, that we dare not say who were to form the ruling or chief Committee. He certainly would rather that this question had been answered by some one else. But as it had been put to him, he would honestly and candidly answer it. He would say, then, that Manchester, from its numbers, its importance, and its situation as the first and most central spinning district in the United Kingdom, but not from any superiority in the intellectual attainments of its people, as Mr. Foster might invidiously attempt to suppose, should be the place where the seat of government ought to be held, and the district from which the materials to compose such a government should be taken. (Hear! hear! from Glasgow.) Mr. Foster had alluded to the annual meeting. Who, he would ask, were to form such a meeting? Was it to be formed from the national Committees, or by representatives from each district, as now assembled? If each district were to attend, then their high-sounding national Committees would be mere nonentities. And they would exist only to please the airy imagination of his friend Mr. Foster. (A laugh.) The annual meetings only were to be the head. He must say, then, that they would have a curious sort of animal. For fifty-one weeks at least, out of the fifty-two in the year, they would have a body without a head. Mr. Foster had foolishly enough asked, where one general Committee was to get its authority.—He would answer that question, by asking Mr. Foster where his national Committees would get their authority?

MR. FOSTER—From the annual meetings.

MR. DOHERTY—From the same source, then, would one general Committee get its authority. So that that argument, like most of those which Mr. Foster had employed on this occasion, was just what his three Committees would prove to be,—good for nothing. He concluded by opposing the motion.

BELFAST heartily concurred with the opinions expressed by Mr. Doherty. One Committee, or whatever name it might have, one head or government, would answer the best purpose in the end.

BOLTON 2 concurred in opinion with Mr. Foster. It would be better to let each country manage its own affairs. He was sure that Bolton would not allow Manchester to govern them as had been proved in the case of the Union already established in England.

GLASGOW 1 said, that they had received instructions to

support such a proposition as that which Mr. Foster had proposed.—If, indeed, they were to have one general Committee only, Manchester certainly appeared to him to be the place where it should be held, and he thought Mr. Doherty was entitled to praise for the candid manner in which he had stated his opinion of this matter.

JOHNSTONE. 1 said, that after all that he had heard, he still thought that one general Committee would answer the best end.—It appeared to him, that Mr. Foster entirely overlooked one material point, which he seemed to promise to himself, in the Establishment of three Committees, namely, that no one district should take precedence of, or be raised above, another. For there could be very little difference between one Committee and three, in that respect. He saw no reason why they could not have as much confidence in one general Committee as three national Committees. Glasgow might think that their plans were as good or better than those of Manchester, and *vice versa*. Thus a sort of breach would be made that might be very hurtful to the general interests of the whole. He would therefore move as an amendment, that the affairs of the Union be managed by one general Committee.

The question was then put, when the original motion was carried by a majority of four.

Owing to a peculiarity in the cotton manufacture, this Union wields a greater power than is possessed by any other in the kingdom. The spinners do not form a greater proportion than one-tenth of those employed in a cotton-mill, but their labour is absolutely necessary to the working of the establishment; consequently, by refusing to work themselves, they force all their fellow-labourers to be thrown out of employment at the same time. Thus, however unwilling nine-tenths of the work-people in a factory may be to strike, they have no power of refusal in the matter, but are subject to the uncontrolled and despotic sway of the remaining tenth, who can order them to cease working, whenever it suits their will and pleasure. This dependence of some workmen on others, of course, exists partially in every business, where there is a division of labour, but in no manufacture where the same quantity of fixed capital is employed (a circumstance which will be shewn hereafter materially to aid the objects of a combination) is the disproportion equally great. As the way in which this power has been exercised, and the general character of spinners' Unions will best be seen in their acts, we proceed to give a history of the principal turn-outs to which they have given rise.

The most extensive and persevering strike, that has ever taken place, is that which occurred in 1810, when all the spinners in all the mills in the neighbourhood of Manchester, including Stockport, Macclesfield, Stayley Bridge, Ashton, Hyde, Oldham, Bolton, and as far north as Preston, simultaneously left their work, and had the strike continued a little longer, the whole of Scotland would have joined it. As it was, 30,000 persons were thrown out of employ; many of them paraded the streets of the above towns during the day, shouting and hooting at the residences of those persons, who, they supposed, were inimical to their cause. Attacks were frequently made on the factories, in defiance of the Police, who were utterly inefficient for protection ; many masters were unable to leave their mills, for fear of their lives, and such workmen as were got to supply the place of the seceders, were held prisoners, in a state of almost continual siege, in the establishments where they worked. The *government* of this strike was carried on by a congress at Manchester, which was formed of delegates sent from all the principal mills. The chief leader in this congress, and, in fact, the chief leader and organizer of the turn-out, was a man named Joseph Shipley, who possessed the greatest influence over the workmen, and appears to have been a perfect Masaniello.* This man, in the words of one of our informants, who, at that time, was a spinner and joined in the strike, was as " a general in the army," the commander of thousands of willing agents, who performed his bidding with the utmost promptitude. It is a curious circumstance, that this person voluntarily came before the Factory Commissioners, in the Manchester district, to give evidence *against* the Short Time Factory Bill : he, however, was not questioned on the subject of his former celebrity, and his evidence is only remarkable for the strong way in which it contradicts the opinion, that children are liable to become deformed by factory labour.

During this turn-out, the men who had struck were supported by the contributions of those who were in work, and the sums so collected amounted

* This man is and long has been a respectable mechanic.

for a considerable period to nearly 1500*l*. weekly, of which Manchester alone paid upwards of 600*l*. This fund was for some time sufficiently large, to enable the congress to make a weekly payment of 12*s*. to the spinners, who had struck, but the contributions, and consequently the allowances that flowed from them, gradually fell off, till they at length ceased altogether, and those who depended on them, were consigned to utter destitution.

The principal object, which the workmen had in view was, to raise the wages in country districts to a level with those in Manchester. In this town, the wages have always been, and of necessity must always be higher than in the surrounding places, for very obvious reasons. It is the mart for the sale of nearly all the yarn and goods that are made in England, here the principal machine makers reside, and it enjoys facilities for obtaining the raw cotton, hardly equalled by any other place in the kingdom. The country masters, being deprived of these advantages, are obliged to reduce the wages of their workmen to a lower rate, as otherwise they would be unable to get the same profit on their capital with their Manchester rivals, *i. e.* the average rate of profit, without which they must cease manufacturing. The ability to get their work performed at lower prices than at Manchester, is the condition of their continuance in the business. At that time 4*d*. was paid in the country parts for spinning a pound of cotton, No. 40, and 4½*d*. in Manchester, and to raise the country wages to this latter sum was the aim of the Union. The attempt met with the most signal failure, and drew with it a punishment, which, if we consider the conduct of those engaged in it, we can ‚hardly think was excessive or undeserved. When the contributions of those in work failed, such of the men as had laid by money in the days of their prosperity, resorted to it for support, and thus the hard-earned savings of perhaps years of industry, were consumed in this hopeless warfare. Furniture, clothes, every article of comfort or convenience that their cottages contained, was then disposed of, and these unhappy victims of their own folly underwent a series of privations, which would appear incredible to those who do not know the force of pride, and the enduring pertinacity, with which the English working classes will not unfrequently remain, what they call, "true to each other." The feeling deserves praise, however we may lament its misdirected energy.

Some minor objects, intended to increase the power of the Union, and fetter the free agency of the masters, were also aimed at in this strike. One of these was to establish a rule, that on any workman being turned away from a mill, a paper containing three names should be presented to the master, and out of these three, he was to be compelled to fill up the vacancy.

The required advance of wages was not obtained in a single instance, and after four months of misery, the men returned to their work, some even accepting employment at the rate of 2d. per pound, instead of 4d., which they had been previously earning; thus submitting to a reduction of 50 per cent. on those wages, to raise which, every thing but existence had been staked.

The Luddite riots in this part of the country, which shortly after took place, originated in great measure in this strike, some of the leaders of which were the persons, who first put the oath of that celebrated machine-breaking confederacy.

The most frequent cause of strikes in the cotton trade has been the introduction of improved machinery, and especially the enlargement of mules, by means of which, the number of spindles a spinner is capable of superintending, has been continually increasing. It should be observed, however, that workmen employed on improved machinery never willingly engage in strikes against it, and when induced so to do, it has always been owing either to the threats or persuasion of others. A master on the introduction of an improved machine into his establishment usually bargains with those he employs at it, to divide the profit of working it between them and himself. He stipulates to pay them less per piece, but still at such a rate, that, owing to the greater power of the machine, they shall be able to take home more earnings at the end of the week, than they would have done, had they worked at the old machinery. Such a bargain is obviously advantageous to the workmen who accept it, but in-

C

jurious to the interests of both masters and men in those manufactories where the improved machine is not introduced. The proprietor of the new method is enabled to undersell his competitors in the market, or if he sells at the same price, to gain more than the ordinary rate of profit, and this always excites the jealousy and hostility of other manufacturers. Hence many of the masters in the cotton trade have been guilty of the disgraceful behaviour of instigating the workmen to turn out against those manufacturers, who were the first to enlarge their mules, suggesting to them that those who used these improved machines, should be compelled to pay at the same rate per piece, as was given in other factories, or that there must be a general fall of wages to those who worked at the unimproved mules. The Union has not been slow in taking the hint, and in fact has frequently acted upon this reasoning, without the suggestions of any but their own body, but it is satisfactory to learn, that these attempts to engross on the part of the workmen all the profits of improved machinery, an object, which if successful, would put a stop to improvements altogether, have always ended in failure.

In the year 1824, all the spinners in Hyde turned out, much against their own wishes, but at the persuasion or dictation of the heads of the Union. The reason given for this step was, that the Hyde spinners were working for wages below the regular rate, inasmuch as they were paid

3s. 7d, per 1000 hanks of 40s., while in other
places 1s. more was given for the same quantity of
work. But the machinery on which the Hyde
spinners worked was so superior, that they could at
these comparatively low prices, earn more weekly
than the neighbouring spinners, who however in-
sisted that their Hyde brethren were paid lower
wages than themselves, and therefore ought to
turn out, whereas it is obvious that they were in
fact paid higher wages than were given elsewhere.
The result of this strike was, that the men, after
enduring the greatest hardships, and costing the
combination between 3000l. and 4000l., came back
to their work at the same wages, which they had
turned out to raise.

In 1829 another serious turn-out took place,
which originated in precisely the same causes as
the one last mentioned,—the introduction of improved machinery. A little before this time,
several masters had erected mules, carrying from
four to five hundred spindles, which enabled the
spinners who worked at them to receive a less sum
in the proportion of three to five for a given quantity of work, and at the same time to earn at least
an equal amount of wages, with those who were employed on the old machinery. Twenty-one mills
and 10,000 persons were thrown idle for six
months by this strike, which, one of the witnesses
of the working classes, who was examined by the
Factory Commission declares, has entailed evils on
the Manchester operatives, which it will be long

before they recover. Many of the men are to this day suffering in destitution the penalty of their folly in 1829, the immediate result of which was their return to work at a reduction of wages from what they were previously receiving, after passing the usual round of privations, and many of them being brought to the verge of starvation. And this was the effect, notwithstanding a contribution, at one time no less than 2s. 9d. weekly, subscribed by each of those in work for their support. In addition to the common outrages, which always accompany strikes, this was sullied with the crime of assassination. Many masters were shot at, but these villainous attempts were unsuccessful, except in the instance of Mr. T. Ashton, one of the most respected of the manufacturers, whose yet unpunished murder attests the excess to which the workmen are capable of proceeding, when impelled by the spirit of combination.

The last great strike amongst the spinners occurred in December 1830, when 3000 spinners at Ashton and Stayley Bridge left their work, by which 52 mills and 30,000 persons were thrown idle for ten weeks, when the men returned to their employment at the same wages, which they had been previously receiving. On this occasion, such was the spirit of riot and insubordination displayed, that it was found necessary to send 1000 additional troops to that part of the country to preserve order, and had it not been for the prompt and judicious measures of Colonel Shaw, the commandant of the district, great destruction of life and property would most probably have ensued.

In Scotland the strikes of the spinners have been fully as frequent and determined as in England, and attended with a greater degree of violence. Mr. Campbell, the sheriff substitute in Renfrewshire, states in his evidence before the combination committee of 1825, that from 1820 to 1823, the Union perpetrated numerous assaults, and even frequently attacked the lives of those individuals who refused to join them; that there were at least four instances of deliberate attempts at assassination, and two to burn cotton mills. This combination, however, was then put down by the resolute conduct of the masters, who united in publishing a notice that they would stop all their mills, till the Union was dissolved, and this, at least for a time, had the desired effect. Not an unusual mode of attack in Scotland on those who oppose the wishes of the Union, is by firing in at the windows during night, and also by throwing vitriol, through which atrocious crime, several have lost their eye-sight, and been otherwise irremediably injured. One man confessed that he had been employed to assassinate four of the masters, who had incurred the displeasure of the Union, and that for the attempt he was to receive 100*l.*, with an addition in case of success. One of the largest cotton manufacturers in Scotland was so annoyed by these combinations in 1820, that he transported part of his capital across the Atlantic, and established a factory at New

York, At present the Spinners' Union in Glasgow is in full vigour and the employers are held in complete control.* No one is allowed to spin without first paying a fine of 1*l.*, and when last year some female spinners had been engaged in Messrs. Dennistoun's mills at one-thirteenth less wages than were given to the men, a deduction, which if we consider the inferiority of their skill was probably fully justified, the Union besieged the factory with a mob of 7000 persons. The proprietors on applying for aid, received the assistance of *two* policemen; they were consequently obliged to come to terms with their assailants, when a compromise was entered into, and they were allowed to employ twelve women, but on the condition that they should be paid at the same rate as the men, and that one of the rioters,

* The following are the latest accounts of outrages arising from strikes. "Two most diabolical scenes of outrage were perpetrated at Glasgow on Monday last (Dec. 16th, 1833). A woman named Mary Macshaffrey, cotton-stretcher, while about entering the close leading to her residence in Charles Street, Calton, was met by some men, one of whom wickedly through into her face, and on her person and clothes a quantity of vitriol, whereby her face was severely injured, one of her eyes was destroyed, and she has since been confined under medical treatment. On the same day about six o'clock in the morning, while Mr. Robert Millar, foreman of the Lancefield spinning company, was on his way from his own house to the company's factory, he was suddenly attacked, and cruelly and severely struck with a heavy and sharp weapon, which cut through the crown of his hat, wounded him on the head, and felled him to the ground. It is supposed that murder was the intent of these ruffians."—*Scotsman*, *Dec.* 21*st*, 1833.

who had been taken prisoner should be permitted to escape.

The committee of the Spinners' Union in Manchester seem invested with almost absolute power, and in the true spirit of despotic tyranny, frequently exercise their authority in ordering strikes without the smallest regard for their fellow-workmen who suffer by them. One instance has been given in the case of the Hyde spinners of their having compelled the men to leave work against their inclination, and the following is a somewhat similar account given by Mr. Chappel, a respectable Manchester manufacturer, of a strike that took place in his mill, and by which he was brought to the verge of ruin. It was given in evidence before the Factory Commission.

I will relate the circumstances of the last turn-out, which took place on the 16th October 1830, and continued till the 17th January 1831. The whole of our spinners, whose average wages were 2l. 13s. 5d., turned out, at the instigation, as they told us at the time, of the delegates of the Union. They said they had no fault to find with their wages, their work, or their masters, but the Union obliged them to turn out. The same week three delegates from the Spinners' Union waited upon us at our mill, and dictated certain advances in wages, and other regulations, to which, if we would not adhere, they said neither our own spinners nor any other should work for us again. Of course we declined, believing our wages to be ample, and our regulations such as were necessary for the proper conducting of the establishment. The consequences were, they set watches on every avenue to the mill night and day, to prevent any fresh hands coming into the mill, an object which they effectually attained, by intimidating some, and promises of support to others which I got into the mill in a caravan, if they would leave their work. Under these circumstances I could not work the mill, and advertised it for sale without receiving any applications, and I also in vain tried to let it. At the end of twenty-three weeks the hands requested to be taken into the mills again on the terms that they had left it, declaring as they had done at first, that the Union alone had forced them to turn out. The names of the delegates that waited on me were Jonathan Hodgins, Thomas Foster, and Peter Madox, secretary to the Union.

What advance of wages did they require?—It was considerable, but I don't remember the exact sum; and the regulations required were, that the men should not be fined for bad work, or for not conforming to the regulations of the mill.

Have you ever had turn-outs before?—Yes, two; in a former turn-out of the spinners, we were waited on by a man named Doherty, and Jonathan Hodgins, two leaders of the Union, who, after examining our wage-book and the machinery on which the men worked, stated that the wages were fair and the machinery good; and they ordered them to their work again.

The funds in possession of this combination are liable to perpetual variations, but at times are very large. Some years ago they boasted of having expended 20,000*l*. in supporting the Unions of other trades, and though this is probably exaggerated, their wealth, when the Association is in full action, cannot be otherwise than considerable, as the weekly subscriptions are constantly going on, and indeed one of the delegates acknowledged to the writer of these lines, that he had in his own person often collected 300*l*. on a Saturday night. Besides the support of their secretaries, delegates, and other incidental expenses, weekly payments to spinners out of work, and for whom there is not sufficient employment, form a constant drain on their funds. The contributions levied by order on those in work are different at different times, varying from 4*d.* or 6*d.*, to 5*s.* or 6*s.* weekly, but some have been known spontaneously to bestow their guineas. The sums are fixed by the Committee, and the decision is always printed on a scrap of paper, a copy of which is sent to each of the members, and serves for a pass-ticket when they attend their meetings. The following is an exact copy of a ticket that was circulated last June.

NOTICE.

TO THE MEMBERS
OF
The Lancashire Trades Unions.

GENTLEMEN,

At a Meeting held at the Princes Tavern, on THURSDAY EVENING, it was unanimously agreed that the contribution should be sevenpence per week for a few weeks, viz :—fourpence for men out of work; one penny for Time Bill,* and twopence for the Grand Lodge expences. All moneys to be paid at the Saint Peter's Tavern, as usual.

Signed by a Committee of EIGHTEEN.

M. Wardle, Printer.

* This alludes to the charges for sending delegates to London, and other expences incurred in supporting the Ten-hour Factory

As might be expected, the members are constantly falling into arrear with their subscriptions, and then by the rules, they are disabled from receiving allowances if they should be thrown out of work. But the Union in such cases cannot in general refuse to support them, as otherwise they declare they shall be compelled to take work for any wages that are offered, and the object sought by the Association, that of keeping up the price of labour, would be defeated.

Surely, if any combination could answer the expectations of the working classes, this would be the one. It has brought the most extensive manufacture in the world under its authority, it has embraced in its power three kingdoms, it exercises by the peculiar nature of the trade, control over ten times its own number of workmen, it has shewn the reality of these pretensions, by keeping thousands out of employ for half a year at a time, every favourable circumstance has concurred to establish its efficiency, and it *has* kept up the rate of wages, yet the members fail to draw from this result one iota of benefit. It is curious and instructive to mark how this consequence has been brought about, how the laws of nature are vindicated in spite of the ablest devices of man to elude them.

Bill of Lord Ashley, in which, as will presently be seen, the Union took a particular interest.

The wages of spinners have been kept up to an average of at least 30s. a week, the prospect of receiving which, has attracted to the business many who might otherwise have betaken themselves to different employments. The work not being sufficient for all, in order to prevent the supernumeraries from beating down the rate of wages, by working under the combination prices, the Union is compelled to make them a weekly allowance for their support; and the subscriptions for this purpose, as well as the other expenses to which they are put in maintaining their association are so heavy, and if they should be thrown out of employment, the chances of regaining it, owing to the number of competitors, so small, that the sum distributed amongst them in wages, is not greater than in other occupations, and their earnings are only nominally high, and really not above the ordinary level.

It may be thought they would be able to attain their object by limiting the number of those admitted to the business, but this they have never been able to do, for one especial reason among others, that the last resort of their power, a strike, invariably introduces new workmen, and thus their end is defeated by the very means taken to gain it. More than 300 persons were instructed in spinning, owing to the turn-out in Ashton in 1825, and Mr. Lees states in his evidence that every general turn-out without exception has ended in a reduction of wages immediately after, on account of the influx of fresh hands causing a superabundance of labour.*

From the evidence relating to the cotton trade taken before the Factory Commission, it appears that the spinners were invariably the most strenuous, and in many cases the only supporters of the Ten-hour Limitation Bill. It is also shewn by the Report of the Commission, that the spinners are nearly the sole employers of the children, and consequently answerable for the cruelty, if any there be in their treatment. Why, then, it may be asked, did they not leave the promotion of this bill to those of their fellow-workmen, who could support it with a decent regard to consistency? Those, who have not penetrated their secret motives, may think this surprising; the circumstance, however, admits of an easy solution.

The effect produced by the Spinners' Union affords an explanation of this anomalous conduct. It has been before stated, that the high wages given in this business, cause a greater number of persons

---

* The following evidence shews the experience of a Manchester workman on the subject of turn-outs.

Have you ever seen a turn-out?—Yes, of all the factories in town. One day they turned-out, and the next day there would be fresh hands in some of the factories working.

Where did these fresh hands come from?—Some came from the country, and some was big piecers what took to spinning.

Did the turn-out succeed?—No; there has been a great many turn-outs, and they have never succeeded. *Evidence of John Pilkington, First Report of Factory Commission.*

to enter it than the trade can employ, and that these superfluous labourers receive a weekly stipend from those who are in work, to prevent them from engaging themselves under the combination prices. The Union calculated, that had the Ten-hour Bill passed, and all the present factories worked one-sixth less time, one-sixth more mills would have been built to supply the deficient production. The effect of this, as they fancied, would have been to cause a fresh demand for workmen; and hence, those out of employ would have been prevented from draining the pockets of those now in work, which would render their wages really as well as nominally high. Here we have the secret source of nine-tenths of the clamour for the Ten-hour Factory Bill, and we assert, with the most unlimited confidence in the accuracy of our statement, that the advocacy of that Bill amongst the workmen, was neither more nor less than a trick to raise wages—a trick, too, of the clumsiest description; since it is quite plain, that no legislative enactment, whether of ten or any other number of hours could possibly save it from signal failure.

One of the most extensive Unions in the kingdom is that formed by the workmen in the Building Trades; it has been peculiarly active during the past year, more especially in the north-western manufacturing districts, and may be said to have exhausted all the resources of combination in an endeavour to gain its end. In the spring of 1833, this body commenced operations in Manchester,

Liverpool, and the neighbouring towns, by serving a requisition on the masters, which demanded an abandonment of the practice of erecting buildings on the system of contracts. Of late years a custom has been introduced of masters in some single department of the Building Trade entering into contracts with those who employed them, by which the contractor bound himself to furnish whatever was required for the construction of the whole edifice. Thus, in the majority of cases, the masters were not immediately engaged by the customers, but by a middleman or agent, who contracted for the erection of the entire building, and hence arose the ignorant outcry among the workmen, of which our history offers such repeated instances, that the due profits of their labour were abstracted by those who were the channels between the producer and the consumer. The masters had been led into this practice by the expressed wish of their customers, to whom it was obviously of the greatest convenience, since it enabled them to obtain the estimate for any work from a single person versed in such calculations, who would be responsible for its completion at the computed price, and it removed the liability to deception and inaccuracy in reckoning the expense, which must have ensued from an application to five or six persons in different trades, unconnected with each other. The masters, however, had no particular desire to continue this system, and most of them complied with the request of their workmen to lay it aside. By this conduct, they shewed their disposition to meet the wishes of the men, and the accommodating spirit by which they were actuated will appear the more strongly, if we consider the imperious mode in which this unreasonable request was made to them; as a specimen of which we give a letter that was sent to Mr. Holmes, a respectable Liverpool builder :—

Liverpool, 11th April, 1833.

Sir,

In consequence of an information received by our Society, that your job in Canning Street is a contract job, we felt ourselves in duty bound to furnish your men at that job with a notice to that effect, and in consequence of such contract to leave that building directly. You will please to understand that previous to their return we require to see your contract in our club-room, to be examined by our Committee appointed for that purpose. When we receive this information we will be happy to be, Sir,

Your most obedient humble Servant,

The Operative Societies of Bricklayers,

Corresponding Secretary.

These concessions, however, so far from reconciling matters between the respective parties, only caused fresh demands to be made on the part of the workmen. The Committee of the Union issued a series of regulations, requiring the masters to abide by certain rules respecting the equalization of wages, the number of apprentices they were to take, the use of machinery, and a variety of other matters, all more or less restrictive, and consequently injurious to the free transaction of business. " The masters, who presumed to disobey these laws, which one of the letters assures them are

'like those of the Medes and Persians, unalter-
able,' were either obliged to submit to the fine,
arbitrarily imposed upon them by the Union, or an
edict was issued by that body to the workmen of
any ' refractory master :' the consequence of which
was, that he found himself at once deserted by his
journeymen, and of course unable to complete the
contracts and other work then in progress."* A
few instances of the mode in which this interference
was exercised will best shew the character of the
Union. Mr. Leatham, a master mason, at Liverpool, having discharged a workman from his employ, the Committee of the Union suspected that
he had done so with a view of punishing the man
for his supposed activity in managing the affairs of
the combination. They accordingly sent him a letter, *ordering* him to appear before the Committee
the same evening, and to give up the name of the
person who had communicated to him the information respecting the part his discharged workman
had taken in the Union, and declaring that the
whole of his men should instantly cease working,
if he refused obedience to this order. Mr. Leatham returned for answer, that the reason imputed
to him for turning away the man, was wholly untrue; but this was deemed unsatisfactory by the
Committee, and the next day he was left without
a single workman. Messrs. Patteson, master
masons, at Manchester, discharged a couple of men

* Extracted from an account printed by the Manchester Masters.

because they had refused to work at a building, at which bricklayers not belonging to the Union were employed. They received in consequence a long remonstrance from the Society, from which the following is an extract :—" It is considered that your conduct toward Robinson and Whitaker, (the men in question) is quite inconsistent, and to be brief, unless you take them again into your employ, on Saturday 8th inst. at one o'clock, all your hands will withdraw themselves on that night from your service, and so remain until you do reinstate the above-mentioned R. and W. And further, that each and every one in such strike shall be paid by you the sum of four shillings per day for every day you refuse to comply." Messrs. Patteson of course refused to comply with this order, and the ensuing day every Unionist in their employ left them.

Many other absurd and tyrannical restrictions on their employers were attempted by the Builders' Union. The Painters published a declaration, which stated that they had " come to one unanimous determination not to work for any gentleman, at any job whatever, who finds his own materials, or does not employ a regular master in the trade to find the same." The lofty and imperious tone assumed in their communications with the masters, brings to mind the grandiloquent edicts of Chinese dignitaries, while it shews the opinion they entertained of the extent of their power. " We consider," says one of these despatches, " that as you have not treated our rules with that deference you ought to

D

have done, we consider you highly culpable, and deserve to be highly chastised." The commands to cease working, issued by the Committees of the Union were in every case implicitly obeyed ; neither the consciousness of the folly of the step, which many must have felt, nor confidence in the goodwill or judgment of an employer, prevented any one from joining in the strike, and in many cases, the mutual respect that had been engendered by thirty and forty years' service under a single master, was found too weak to prevent a workman assisting in these tyrannical proceedings against his employer.

Under these circumstances, the masters, finding that concession was of no avail, and only served to encourage fresh and more unreasonable demands, while serious impediments were placed in the way of their business, determined to employ no workmen, except such as should sign a declaration, that they did not belong to a Trades' Union. The men, as might have been expected, refused to comply with this demand, in consequence of which a general turn-out ensued, and for more than six months the vast building operations, commonly carried on amidst the immense and increasing population of Manchester, Liverpool, and places in the vicinity, were almost entirely suspended. Some idea may be formed of the magnitude of the effects resulting from this proceeding, when it is stated, that the consumption of bricks in Liverpool was instantly reduced from a million weekly to twenty thousand ;

and a master builder, who was called as a witness in a prosecution that took place in that town a few months back, stated, in the course of his examination, that he had paid 11,000*l*. less in timber duties, and 800*l*. less in duties on bricks that year than the year before, owing to the stoppage in the erection of buildings. The returns to the revenue from the excise in the quarter succeeding the strike, shew a decrease, on comparison with the same quarter in the preceding year, of 183,740*l*. ; and many ominous reasons were given at the time to account for this deficiency. The conduct of the Builders' Union readily and satisfactorily explains the cause of the diminution ; for if we consider that the excise on bricks of the poorest description is 5*s*. 10*d*. per thousand, and that the duty in Liverpool would on the reduced consumption of this class of building materials have fallen off 3,430*l*. weekly ; that this was the result on a single article in a single town, it will be seen that this turn-out fully explains the reduction that took place in the quarter in question ; indeed, it seems probable, that had it not been for this circumstance, the revenue returns in the excise would have shewn a considerable excess.

The little excuse that can be made for this conduct of the workmen on the score of wages, will appear from the fact, that the masters had made no attempt whatever to reduce them, or to interfere with the usual privileges and practices of any one in their employ, that the earnings of the journey-

men in the building trades had never been less than
24s. weekly during the last twenty years, and had
sometimes exceeded this sum ; moreover, that at
the very time of the strikes, the wages of the bricklayers had been increased 3s. weekly, and that
many of this class of men were in the habit of
earning 35s. a week, during the summer months,
by working longer hours than usual. If we consider these wages with reference to the quantity of
necessaries they will purchase at different times,
and this is the only correct mode of estimating
their rise or fall, they will appear to have enormously advanced, and in fact nearly doubled, as
the following table of prices of provisions at Manchester for the two extremities of the twenty years
will shew .—

	1813.		1833.	
	s.	d.	s.	d.
Flour (good seconds) per dozen pounds,	4	2 — 2		2
Butcher Meat, good, per pound, .	0	8½— 0		6½
Do. coarse, per pound, .	0	6½— 0		5
Bacon, per pound, . .	0	11 — 0		6
Cheese, per pound, . .	0	9 — 0		7
Potatoes, per load of 240 pounds, .	12	0 — 4		6
Butter, per 112 pounds, . .	126	0 —90		0
Soap, per pound, . .	0	9 — 0		6
Coals, per pound, . .	0	8 — 0		5¾
Salt, per pound, . .	0	3 — 0		0¼
Candles, per pound, . .	1	0 — 0		6

If we measure their wages in clothing they will
appear to have advanced in a still greater ratio.
We do not possess the prices for 1813, but 1810
will serve this purpose nearly as well. We ex-

tract the following from the Report of the Factory Commission, which has also furnished part of the preceding table :—

	1810.	1833.
	s. d.	s. d.
Linen, per yard,	1 8 —	0 9
Strong Calico, per yard,	0 10 —	0 4
Printed Calico, per yard,	2 2 —	0 7

The Masters endeavoured to procure fresh workmen from other parts of England, but their efforts in this way seem to have been attended with little success, owing to the intimidation practised by the Union workmen. The shops of the masters were constantly watched by picquets of three or four men, who were relieved at certain intervals, and who generally succeeded in preventing by menaces any new labourers applying for employment, and if any such were by any means engaged, the buildings where they worked were surrounded by Unionists, who, by hooting, and other more effectual modes of annoyance, endeavoured to impede the progress of the work.

In the mean time, the workmen in the building trades throughout the whole of England, instigated, probably, by their Lancashire brethren, were seized with an universal spirit of combination, and determined to form one general Union. A scheme of representative government was accordingly drawn up, members were chosen in the different counties, and in September last, the inhabitants of Manchester were astonished by the holding of a *Builders'*

Parliament in their town. But little secrecy was observed in their proceedings, and they seemed even to court attention; two hundred and seventy-five delegates, representing, as they declared, a constituency exceeding thirty thousand, walked arm in arm through the streets, when they went to open the session. Their dress and mode of living, both of the best description, displayed the resources of the body; but the necessary expenses which were incurred in paying salaries to the members, and for other purposes, amounting, as we are informed, to 3,000*l.*, have considerably cooled their zeal for repeating this absurd experiment, and the folly of a Builders' Parliament has probably been enacted for the first and last time.

The delegates, however, anticipated many returns of their session; they passed a resolution, which declared the expediency of having some central representative body, to which all the members of the trade should owe allegiance; they also enacted a variety of laws which were to regulate the future proceedings of their commonwealth, and whose provisions were to be obeyed in every part of England.

The next important occurrence in the history of this combination, was the proposal to found in some spot, near the centre of our island, a Guildhall, which should contain rooms for public meetings, and for other purposes of the Union, and from which their government, established in all the

forms of regal power, was to issue laws to its subjects in other parts of the empire. Birmingham
was chosen as the most convenient situation, and
the 5th of December last saw the commencement
of the design. On that day, deputations from the
different divisions of the Building Trades march-
ed in procession, accompanied by banners and
music, through the streets of the great northern
workshop, and proceeded to lay the first stone of
an edifice, whose grandeur *on paper* shewed the
expectations they entertained of their future great-
ness. The design is truly magnificent; the first
floor contains a room for public meetings, whose
dimensions are 78 feet long by 30 feet wide, and
24 feet high, and on whose adornment all the
efforts of the painter's and carver's art are to be
lavished. The other parts of the building are appropriated to rooms for committees, schools, and
lectures, and such labourers as are unemployed in
consequence of strikes are engaged in relays for the
execution of the work.

Nothing can be more praiseworthy than some of
the professed objects of this institution. Schools
are to be provided for the education of the members' children, and evening lectures are to be given
to adults, who are to receive instruction in all the
theoretical principles of their trade, for which purpose, models, drawings, and every necessary scien-
tific apparatus are to be obtained.

Were it possible to leave out of view certain circumstances appertaining to this and similar socie-

ties, we might hope that the germs of good, which they contain, would eventually be productive of some real benefit to the labouring classes,—that the members of this institution might in time learn the true extent of their power, and the advantages which are really within their reach, and that at length, taught wisdom by experience, they might reject the evil, and retain only the beneficial part of their design. But when we contemplate the radical absurdity of the main object of the confederation, the foolish spirit in which it has acted, the extravagant imbecility of the publications which propound its doctrines, and above all, when we look at the character of the persons who take the chief lead in its management, it seems as reasonable to expect grapes from thistles, as good to result from a combination, sullied by such folly, and conducted by such agents. Through some unhappy fatality, the working classes seem generally to have chosen for their leaders, those who, by character and accomplishment, are least fitted for the station.

The Lancashire workmen persisted in their strike for more than six months, when, there being no prospect of the masters acceding to their proposals, the combination was voted a nuisance, and forsaken by all, and they returned in penitence to their employers, requesting work on the old terms. But they paid sufficiently dear for their folly. During the best part of the year, when their labour was most in request and their wages at the highest point, they had remained idle, living on the scanty allowance doled out to them by the Union funds. The sum spent in making these allowances approached 18,000*l*., and as the payments to workmen, who have turned out, never average at the most more than one-fourth of their earnings, four times this sum, or 72,000*l*. was the loss, which the working builders sustained in pursuit of their insane project. They had hoped that their masters would have been willing and eager to re-employ them when the strike was at an end. But even this small consolation was in a great measure groundless, as the event proved. They had refused work when there was work in abundance for all ; in consequence of this refusal, many of the buildings were discontinued, and the places of some of the men were supplied by fresh labourers brought from distant parts, and also by the introduction of machinery : so that the applications for employment could not be granted. Every circumstance seemed to concur in increasing the misery of their condition. By their long cessation from work, habits of idleness, and not a little increase of immorality had ensued,—in the false hope of attaining their object, they had endured deprivations only second to actual starvation, and now when the day of forced repentance had come, the still further degradation of pauperism awaited them. The failure of the strike was complete, and the disastrous consequences that resulted from it have taught a lesson to the Lancashire work-people, which, it is to be hoped, they will never forget.

The following is the oath, which every member was required to take, and which was administered with the ceremonial accompaniments detailed in the account of the Yorkshire Unions :—" I do, before Almighty God and this Loyal Lodge, most solemnly swear, that I will not work for any master that is not in the Union, nor will I work with any illegal* man or men, but will do my best for the support of wages ; and most solemnly swear to keep inviolate all the secrets of this Order ; nor will I ever consent to have any money for any purpose but for the use of the Lodge and support of the trade ; nor will I write or cause to be wrote, print, mark, either on stone, marble, brass, paper, or sand, any thing connected with this Order, so help me, God, and keep me steadfast in this my present obligation ; and I further promise to do my best to bring all legal men that I am connected with into this Order; and if ever I reveal any of the rules, may what is before me plunge my soul into eternity."

As a desire to put an end to the contract system —the source of so many other Unions—was the first and main object of this, and as even among persons in a higher rank, those, who perform the

* " Illegal," in the language of the Unions, generally means contrary to their own laws, and has no reference to the law of the land. Wherever the term is used in this work, the context will easily decide its signification.

office of intermediate agents between the producer
and consumer, are not unfrequently regarded as
injurious—diminishing the profits of both, with
benefit only to themselves,—it may not be improper in this place to state the real utility, which
society derives from the existence of this class.
Their business owes its origin and depends for its
continuance on the facilities for mutual intercourse
which they afford to those parties, between whom
they interpose. The consumer buys woollen cloth
from the shopkeeper, who purchases it from the
manufacturer, who pays the weaver for making it.
The shopkeeper and manufacturer both make a
profit on the article, as it passes through their
hands, and this profit, it is said, the weaver may
secure for himself, or at least share with the consumer, by dispensing with the system of agency,
which now forms a connecting link for the two.
Yet there can be no doubt that both weaver and
consumer would lose by such a change in the
method of communication, and in like manner,
the shopkeeper would be injured by endeavouring
to get his wares without the intervention of the
manufacturer. Those, who form the channels of
intercourse between different classes of persons,
only hold their existence on the tenure of their
utility. To quarrel with the expense, which they
occasion, is as absurd as it would be to object to
the cost of the pipes, which convey water to our
houses, when their absence would necessitate the
expenditure of, perhaps, a hundred times that sum,

in sending to the river or fountain for each gallon
that is wanted. The objection implies, that each
man would be better off by dispensing with the
assistance of others, that every one ought to do
every thing he wants for himself, and that division
of labour, the great benefit of civilization, is a
positive evil.

An apparent sanction to this opinion is sometimes given by cases, whose real nature will best
be seen and illustrated in an example. Prior to
the formation of docks in London, the builders
used to supply themselves with timber, from a class
of middlemen called yard-keepers, who bought
the article from the importing merchant, and disposed it for sale in yards, which they kept for this
purpose. The convenience of docks enabled the
builder and the merchant to conduct their intercourse without the intervention of any third person,
and both were of course benefited by the change.
This result would give occasion to those who gene-
ralize from single facts, half understood, to dilate
on the evils of the agency system, and the advantage that would be derived from abolishing it
altogether in every case, whereas it is clear, that
in this instance, the middleman was useful when
the docks were not made; for he supplied the
want of them by a substitute, which, though bad
in comparison with a dock, was found beneficial to
the merchant and builder, and consequently increased their profits, instead of diminishing them.
It is true, that for some time after the completion

of the docks, the new mode of conducting the builder's business was not discovered or adopted, and the yard-keepers consequently found employment, when their existence, in reference to the building occupations, was really needless; but this only amounts to the assertion, that the most profitable method of carrying on the trade was not at once found out and recognized, nor is it easy to see, how, without the aid of inspiration, any thing whatever, can attain to sudden perfection.

But a notion, not unlike the former, is abroad among the working classes, that they will be able to save great part of the expense now incurred in the transmission of the products of their labour to the consumer, by having agents of their own. To do this, they must become capitalists, they must possess money sufficient to rent warehouses and shops, and then if they sold their wares for less than other tradesmen, they must either make less than the average profit on their capital, or their own wages must fall; in either case, they would be sufferers. The Derby work people are at this moment erecting factories by the aid of subscriptions, collected among themselves, and also from brother Unionists in all parts of England, hoping by these means to draw to their own body the profit, which has been hitherto taken by their masters. Doubtless, they may thus get the common rate of profit on the capital they lay out—if they get less, they will not obtain what is justly their due—if more, their own wages must be reduced. In no way can they increase their gains beyond that, which is the proper return for the money they may invest. That they should do this—that their efforts to become capitalists should be successful—that they should be able to work with benefit to themselves in factories established by their own money, is most ardently to be wished, and every judicious friend to the working classes would rejoice in the triumph of this scheme. We may doubt the feasibility of the project, or whether a joint-stock company of this description, if feasible, would be found to answer expectation, but we have no doubt whatever of the benefit that would result from its success, both to the workmen, who should join in it, and to the community at large. One thing, however, we would impress on the projectors, that strikes cannot assist, but, on the contrary, must greatly impede their end, by checking the influx of the subscriptions, which are to make up the requisite amount of capital.

Having given in the preceding pages some account of the Unions that have been formed in the North-Western manufacturing districts, we proceed to sketch the effects that have resulted from the spirit of combination in the clothing parts of Yorkshire.

On the repeal of the combination laws in 1824, the Yorkshire workmen employed in the woollen cloth trade endeavoured to establish a Union. They, however, failed to accomplish their object at that time, as the society they formed, died or fell into insignificance shortly after its birth. The combinations that have lately been doing such extensive mischief in that part of the kingdom were not set on foot till about three years ago, and at first only embraced those workmen employed in what is technically termed the "manufacturing" of woollen cloth, viz. slubbers, spinners and weavers.

One of the largest manufacturing establishments in Leeds, that belonging to Messrs. Gott was the first to feel the power of the Union. The proprietors had at that time just completed an enormous building intended for the weaving of fine woollen cloth; all the costly machinery adapted to this purpose had been purchased and erected, every necessary arrangement for commencing the business had been made, when all the weavers, to the number of 210 turned out. The men declared that they were paid lower wages than were given by other Leeds manufacturers, which was positively untrue; as the wages given in this establishment were not exceeded by any other in the town, and averaged 17s. weekly. There can be little doubt that the real motive which prompted this strike, was the wish of the Union to make a trial of their new-born authority, and to see whether they could not raise the general rate of wages by compelling one manufacturer to accede to their wishes, in the hope that the rest would then be induced to follow his example. This particular establishment was doubtless chosen for the attempt, as from the large fixed capital, which its proprietors had lately invested in buildings and machinery, it was supposed that the loss consequent on its lying idle, would quickly force a submission to the demands of the Union.

For some weeks the required advance of wages was resisted, till at length those men who continued at their work were subject to such treatment on entering and leaving the factory, being hooted, pelted, and annoyed in other ways, (which, though not direct violations of law, are almost as effectual as personal violence,) that the proprietors, receiving no support or countenance from other manufacturers, were induced to accede to the terms proposed. The men, however, were disappointed in obtaining all the advantage they looked for, as Messrs. Gott determined only to take back sufficient weavers to work the looms in the old part of their establishment, leaving their newly erected building unused. They soon after disposed of all the machinery it contained, and this magnificent structure, no less than 136 yards in length, now stands in useless grandeur, untenanted by a single piece of machinery, or one human being, a melancholy monument of the disastrous effect consequent on the first exercise of power by the Leeds' Union.

The success which followed this contest led to a coalition of the Union with the workmen engaged in the various processes of " finishing," as well as " milling or fulling" woollen cloth, and since that period, the trade has hardly ever been free from strikes, and the workmen have wielded an almost irresistible power over the property of their masters.

The next step of the Union was to draw up a list of wages to be paid for spinning, weaving, &c., which was published in the newspapers, and also on sheets of paper, for the purpose of being transmitted to the mill-owners and small manufacturers. This document was headed " A scale of prices *to be observed* by mill-owners, manufacturers, &c.," and had appended to it some regulations as to the admission of boys, and the proportion in which they were to be employed relatively to the number of adults. The workmen were then ordered by the Committee of the Union to demand of their respective employers, compliance with this scale of wages, care being taken that the manufacturers should be successively applied to for this purpose, in order that there might be less chance of any general resistance on their part, and that the combination might not have too many on its hands at once. The far greater part of the masters acceded to these demands, and their names were carefully set forth in the three newspapers published at Leeds.

The workmen contended that this scale was not a rise of wages, but only what they termed an " equalization" of them, it being a principal object of their association to compel the masters to pay every operative, good or bad, an equal sum for his

E

labour. But in reality, the scale did sanction a rise of wages, for although no one item in it could be challenged as an advance, inasmuch as some one manufacturer paid the quoted price for the kind or quantity of work specified, yet no one manufacturer paid a price equal to the scale for all the descriptions of work to which it referred. Many masters might be pointed out who gave the wages demanded by the Union for weaving, but then they paid less for spinning, or if they paid the required rate for spinning, they gave less for weaving. Calculated by the whole expense of manufacturing, all were pretty much on a par as to the wages paid on the yard of cloth, but the Union took as its standard for spinning the prices of those who paid the highest for that process, and the same for other sorts of work, so that compliance with their scale was tantamount to an advance of wages.

But in spite of this advance, the workmen failed to gain the expected advantage from it, as the masters were prevented by the state of the market from making beyond a certain quantity of cloth, and that only of the superior qualities, while paying the advanced rate of wages ; they consequently either sent their yarn to be woven in the neighbouring villages, (as it was in the weaving chiefly that the advance was required), where wages are always lower than at Leeds, or stopped part of their works entirely, and thus a great many of the men were thrown permanently out of employ, who of course had to be supported by those who got work. Some of the manufacturers managed to escape the losses they would otherwise have sustained by making alterations in spinning the yarns and setting the webs, by which latter phrase is to be understood the fixing of the geer or reed in which the cloth is woven, and which varies from 36 to 110 portions of 38 threads each. By the alterations made, the manufacturer got the same quantity of yarn converted into cloth of the same nominal quality as before, and for the same cost per yard. For instance, if he had been paying previous to the promulgation of the scale 2s. for an 80 geer, and the scale fixed 2s. 3d. as the price of weaving per string, he would weave the same quality of wool in a 76 geer, at 2s., making such alterations in the spinning of the yarn as were requisite. The Union made new regulations to meet this contrivance, which were counteracted by fresh evasions on the part of the manufacturers, and thus a war of cunning was carried on between masters and men, in which the latter were sometimes beaten, and in some instances they voluntarily requested their employers to return to their old system and prices. The worst of this was, that the goodness of the cloth was impaired by the alteration of the geer and spinning, and thus the public had to pay in the deteriorated quality of the cloth they purchased, and our foreign trade was doubtless injured by these futile attempts of the workmen to raise their wages beyond the natural level.

These successes, partial and profitless though they were, at least shewed that the Union did possess power, and emboldened it to proceed a step further in its exactions. It now commenced a system of interference in the management of the manufacturers' business, by requiring them, in case of a contraction of their scale of production, not to discharge any of their workmen, but to keep every loom and jenny going, dealing out the work, however small might be its quantity, in equal proportions to their men. This demand being partially complied with, the masters were next desired not to stop a single one of the machines used in the processes preparatory to spinning, though, from the falling off of their orders, it should not be necessary to keep them all in work. This useless subdivision of the work to be done would have seriously damaged the cloth, besides inflicting a great loss on the manufacturer, by compelling him in some cases to keep two steam-engines going, when one was sufficient; in consequence, this demand was vigorously resisted, and the workmen, probably finding that it was not likely to benefit them, withdrew this unreasonable claim.

It has been stated above, that when a master had been compelled to raise the wages of his men, he employed a much fewer number in Leeds, and sent the greater part of his work to be done in the neighbouring villages. As this counteracted the object of the Union, it was determined to prevent it, by ordering the manufacturers to get all their weaving and spinning done in Leeds alone, and one master was actually induced to sign a paper, by which he pledged himself, to weave and spin all the cloth he made on his own premises, at the prices fixed by the Union. The result, however, proved any thing but a triumph to his men, as he immediately reduced his manufacture nearly two-thirds, and took in work instead from the country manufacturers to scribble and slubb, and consequently his weavers' earnings were reduced from 17s. to 7s. per week, and his spinners from 27s. to 10s. After three months' endurance, his workmen petitioned him to recommence manufacturing as before, and proposed a scale of prices only a shade above those which he had formerly paid, but he refused compliance with their wishes.

One of the latest strikes originated in an attempt of the Union to compel a master to get all his cloth woven in Leeds, and on his refusal, the Committee declared that they would stop his country weavers, as well as his town ones, by ordering a turn-out of all the men who were employed by him in Leeds, in preparing the wool previous to its being sent into the country. This was accordingly done, and 500 persons were instantly thrown out of employ; but the works were not quite stopped, as the manufacturer happened to employ a considerable number of workhouse children, who were learning the business in his factory. The Union determined to prevent this partial escape from their power, and having found that one of the overseers was a butcher, they threatened him with a loss of all his custom, if he did not prevent the children working in the interdicted factory. The overseer yielded to these menaces, the children were withdrawn from their employment, and thus the parish had to pay the whole charges of their maintenance, because such was the pleasure of the Leeds' Union.

The tyranny of the Association now knew no bounds; and the Committee, like all ignorant men in the possession of authority, for which they are wholly unfitted by intellectual acquirement, ran riot in their power, and frequently exercised it in the mere wantonness of passion and caprice. They determined to change the mode of paying wages, and that in future each man should not be paid by the piece, as was the general practice, but by a weekly allowance of their own fixing. An instance of the way in which this determination was enforced, will shew the character of their proceedings. The overlookers of a large factory were *summoned* before the Committee, and ordered to pay the work people in their establishment at the rate of 21s. a week, and not by the piece. Upon this, the overlookers produced the books of the mill, and proved to the Committee that the men were then earning 23s. a week at piece-work, and therefore, that to comply with the demands of the Union, would be to reduce the men's wages. The Committee answered, that the master was cheated by his men, and that their orders must be obeyed.

They were obeyed, and at the end of the week, the master discovered that his work-people had only turned off as much work as was worth 15*s.* at the usual prices. Thus the manufacturer, his men, and the public, were all injured by this oppressive proceeding. The absence of the stimulus of being paid according to the work done, was doubtless one cause of the relaxed exertion of the men, but we suspect that the large decrease in this instance, was owing to the express commands of the Committee, given in pursuance of the policy which influenced them in advocating the Ten-hour Factory Bill, viz. to diminish the quantity of goods brought to market, and thus, as they foolishly supposed, to raise the rate of wages.

Another manufacturer, who had been forced in the way just mentioned, to change the mode of paying his men, was treated with an additional instance of oppression, which could hardly be exceeded by an Eastern despot. As soon as he discovered the loss he was sustaining on account of the small quantity of work performed by his men on the plan of weekly wages, he naturally complained to the Committee, upon which he was ordered to keep *no books*; and to this extraordinary command he was compelled to yield submission.

As the Union has never published the regulations, which it wishes to establish with respect to the employment of its members, masters have often unconsciously infringed them. In these cases the innocent delinquent is visited with summary punishment, with as little scruple or mercy as if he acted from design. Perhaps, in the middle of the week, when every thing apparently is going on as usual, a signal is suddenly given by one of the men, every one of whom, without mentioning the grievances, will instantly leave his work, and in five minutes the factory will be deserted. In ordering these strikes the policy of the Union has seemingly been to embarrass the manufacturer as much as possible,—to stop him at the busiest season, when delay in the completion of his orders, or in the prosecution of the various processes of manufacturing could least be endured. One manufacturer was punished by a turn-out of eight days continuance, because he discharged a workman for negligence, and changed an overlooker from one department to another.

The most effectual mode of compelling every workman to join the combination, consisted in proscribing any factory where one of these " *black sheep*," as the non-Unionists were called, was employed. In one case, a large body of men struck for several weeks on account of one of their fellow-workmen refusing to join the Association, and when they at length compelled compliance, the man was forced to pay a fine of 10*s.*, besides all arrears of subscription to the funds of the Union, reckoning from the time of its formation. As delay in paying his weekly contributions to the Union Fund subjects any member to be considered a " black sheep," the Committee are enabled by the threat of executing this rule, to use the masters as tools in enforcing the punctual payment of their demands. A manufacturer has sometimes been obliged to threaten the discharge of a contumacious Unionist, if he did not pay up his arrears of subscription to the Combination. A workman sometimes incurs the irrevocable displeasure of the Union, and then the condition of an Eastern Pariah is not more miserable. No master dare employ him, and the obnoxious person has in consequence been reduced to destitution, or compelled to leave the country.

Various rules were laid down with respect to the admission of apprentices into any manufactory, the number being regulated by that of the adults employed, and none allowed to enter as such above the age of fifteen. The number of boys was also limited on a similar principle, and if any one of them was employed on work usually performed by a man, he was to be paid man's wages. No one was allowed to work at any of the trades exercised by their body, unless he had served a regular apprenticeship to them, nor could a workman leave one department of the business to enter another; a weaver could not become a spinner, nor a gigger a shearman, and *vice versâ.* Thus an excess or deficiency of workmen in any particular employment could not be easily remedied, and the free circulation of labour, to the detriment chiefly of the operatives themselves, was seriously impeded.

As to the introduction of new or improved machines, intended to economise labour, no attempt has yet been made by the manufacturers on a scale sufficiently large to develope the feeling of the Unionists respecting this nice point. But from some indications that have been given, there can be no doubt that such an attempt would be strenuously resisted by them. In one manufactory an improved gig, a machine used in raising the cloth, was lately introduced from Manchester, with the design of substituting its operation for one entirely manual. Upon this, delegates were immediately despatched from Leeds to Manchester, who waited on the inventor, and told him that if he sent out any more of these machines, the Union would prevent their use, by ordering a strike against any master, who should introduce them. The reason of their peculiar hostility to this invention was, probably, because it would supersede a class of workmen, the last relic of the croppers, who, in 1811 and 1812, caused so much disturbance in the West Riding. The members of this class are the most restless men in the cloth trade, and the ringleaders in almost all strikes.

The regulation of these various matters implies, of necessity, the assumption of a judicial character, and the Committee have taken upon themselves to decide in all disputes between the workmen and their employers. When a man is discharged, no matter for what cause, or has any real or fancied grievance, he instantly lays his complaint before the Committee, and demands redress. Their only means of enforcing it is by ordering a strike, which has thus sometimes taken place on the most absurd and frivolous pretences. The leaders of the Association are frequently aware of the injustice and impolicy of the course they are pursuing, and of the unfounded nature of the charges, for which they have been induced to sanction a turn-out. But the constitution of the body is essentially democratic : the authority of the Committee is little more than nominal, and they are perpetually controlled by the clamours and violence of the constituency. A strike is always popular; those who demand one and meet with a refusal, instantly begin to form parties and raise murmurs against their leaders ; while the calmest and most reasoning of the members are suspected of a bias in favour of the masters. Consequently, opposition to the proposal is always dangerous, and the power of the Committee being thus confined to measures of active hostility, and nearly useless for purposes of restraint, may be said to exist almost wholly for evil.

The organization of the workmen in the stuff and worsted trades, the manufacturing processes in which are totally distinct from the woollen, is as perfect, and formed on precisely the same principles as that which has been described. The most remarkable strike that has arisen from this Union is that which took place last year in the establishments belonging to Messrs. Hindes and Derham, by which all their work-people, exceeding 1000 in number, were thrown out of employ. This turn-

out ended in the complete discomfiture of the men,
and it forms the only instance we are aware of in
these trades, of a manufacturer having single-
handed defied the whole power of one of the most
extensive Unions in England, and at length gaining
the victory. This result is mainly attributable to
the peculiar locality of the mills belonging to the
firm, one of which was situated in Dolphinholme,
a small hamlet, seven miles from Lancaster, a
second in Leeds, and a third in Bradford. The
first of these was the chief scene of the dispute, and
to its distance from any large town, and facility of
getting workmen from the neighbouring agricultural district, the successful resistance must in a
great measure be ascribed   The little reason there
was for a strike ou the score of wages, may be
learnt from the fact, that the earnings of forty wool-
combers in the year previous to their turning out,
averaged 41*l*. 11*s*. 9½*d*. each man, or 15*s*. 11¾*d*.
weekly; and that the average earnings of the
sixty-three families employed in the establishment
for the same time, consisting of four persons and a
minute fraction in every family, were 87*l*. 19*s*. 6*d*.
Every mode of annoyance which the Union could
devise was put in practice on this occasion. The
workmen lived in cottages belonging to their employers, and obstinately refused to quit, when the
proprietors were compelled to bring no less than
forty-seven actions of ejectment at the Lancaster
assizes, in order to obtain possession. Funds for
the support of the men were subscribed by their

fellow-workmen in every part of the country, as will be seen by the following extract from the books of the Union, which gives the receipts and payments to Dolphinholme from September 11th, 1832, to February 2nd, 1833.

PAID TO DOLPHINHOLME.

	£.	s.	d.
From Kendal	27	16	0
Leeds	58	5	11
Halifax	85	0	0
No. 2 Lodge, No. 2 District.	5	0	0
*Bradford	1822	10	3½
Other sums from Keighley, Halifax, and Kidderminster . . . . . }	59	9	8½
Total paid to Dolphinholme £2058	1	11	

Besides the sums disbursed in maintaining in idleness those who had struck, and which are not all given in the preceding account, many other heavy expenses were incurred. Among these we may mention the sending the whole of the Dolphinholme workmen across the country to Leeds, and on the whole, we have reason to believe, that 4000*l.* is beneath the sum, which the Union expended in this unsuccessful contest.

This strike was the cause of the invention of the wool-combing machine, which wholly superseded the labour of that class of men, who were the chief ringleaders in this affair, and which has struck a blow at their combination, that it can never re-

* This large subscription is owing to Bradford being the principal seat of the worsted trade.

cover. The highest credit is due to Messrs. Hindes and Derham for the spirit with which they resisted the tyranny it was attempted to impose on them, the oppressive nature of which will appear by one demand that was made in writing, by which they were required to dismiss seven persons who had become obnoxious to the Union. Compliance with this request would have deprived them of the control necessary to carry on their business; and not less tact and conduct was displayed in opposing these despotic proceedings, than enterprise in discovering a mode, by which not only the proprietors of these works, but other manufacturers in the trade must eventually free themselves in great measure from the dictation of those they employ.

The constitution and governing power of the various Unions that exist in the clothing districts, are established on the same principles; therefore the description of one, the Combination of the stuff and worsted operatives, will be sufficient to give a general insight into the way in which their business is conducted. For the purposes of this Union the country is divided into "districts," each of which contains a certain number of "lodges," or separate clubs of workmen. Every district elects a governing committee, and also sends delegates, whose numbers are proportionate to the quantity of "lodges" it comprises, to what is called the "grand lodge," held twice a year. At this "grand lodge" meeting, the "grand committee," or council of direction, is chosen, consisting of seven delegates, which forms in theory the supreme governing power of the Union, and which has alone the right of deciding upon strikes, when the object is to raise wages; to prevent reductions, the district authorities are empowered to order strikes. The place of meeting of the "grand lodge" is annually changed : the delegates, who form it are paid according to the distance they have to travel; those who belong to the district in which it holds its sittings, receive 3s. 6d. daily, besides their dinners, those who come from other districts, 5s. and dinners, and 2d. per mile if they travel 100 miles or under, if they travel more than 100 and not beyond 200 miles, 3d. per mile, and exceeding that distance 4d. per mile. A monthly report is drawn up by each lodge, which contains an account of all its receipts and disbursements, and also of its general condition. These reports are communicated to the Secretary of the "grand lodge," by whom they are distributed to the several districts. Full members are required by the rules to pay 1s. entrance money, and 3d. weekly, and are entitled to receive, when they have struck work, a weekly allowance of 7s. besides 1s. for a wife, and 1s. for each child under 10, that is unemployed. The constitution and practice of the society is set forth with greater minuteness in the rules given in the appendix.

A perusal of the rules by which this, and other Unions profess to be guided, will give a very faint and inaccurate idea of their operations. It is to be doubted, whether any of them have ever accurately defined the nature, grounds and extent of their demands on behalf of their members; new regulations are constantly framed on the occurrence of junctures, which suggest an object to be attained; the law is made for the occasion; success encourages new demands, and they are thus tempted gradually to extend their encroachments to a degree wholly inconsistent with the natural freedom of the manufacturer, and utterly destructive to the interests of both capitalist and labourer.

The workman, who enters one of these Unions, on the expectation that their rules are or can be observed, will find himself wofully deceived. He will have to pay more than they enact, and to receive less. By the regulations of the combination, of which an account has been given, a member has to pay 3d. weekly, and to be paid 9s. or 10s. when out of work, while in practice, the weekly contribution has been frequently 1s., 2s., and sometimes even 5s., and the allowance, when on a strike, the merest pittance that can suffice for subsistence. The power, which the rules give to the Committees of deciding on strikes, is perpetually encroached on by the men; and even when the Committee have openly declared that a turn-out has been wholly unjustified by the circumstances of the case, and contrary to the rules, the men have been allowed to draw their subsistence from the Union. When a strike takes place, and any of those who join in it are much in arrear with their subscriptions, they are disabled by the rules from receiving any assistance from the general funds. The enforcing of this regulation is obviously necessary to prevent bankruptcy, and yet it never can be enforced, for the manifest reason, that a refusal to support those who are in arrear, would compel them to accept employment at any price, and the object of a turn-out would be defeated. Hence the Union never has any considerable sum at command, and has often been brought to the verge of ruin from the exhaustion of its funds. This will be seen by the following account, taken from the books of a Combination in the stuff and worsted trade : it includes the pecuniary transactions of the Society from September 11th, 1832, to February 2nd, 1833. The payments are for strikes at the different places mentioned ; the large sum opposite Dolphinholme, arose from the turn-out that has been mentioned in a previous page.

CASH ACCOUNT,

Commencing Sept. 11th, 1832, and ending Feb. 2nd, 1833.

Dr.	£.	s.	d.	Cr.	£	s	d
Rec. from Kidderminster	25	0	0	Paid to Keighley	15	0	0
Halifax	545	0	0	Dolphinholme	1882	0	0
Keighley	536	0	0	Leeds	255	0	0
Bradford	1822	10	3½	Bradford	794	17	9
Balance due to Treasurer	18	7	5½				
Total	2946	17	9	Total	2946	17	9

The ceremonies of admission into the Yorkshire Unions are of the most awful description ; oaths are administered, binding the takers of them in the strongest terms that language can supply, to forward to the utmost of their power the objects of the combination : every accessary device is employed to strike terror into those who go through these inaugural rites, and with such success, that workmen have sometimes been unable to recover their proper senses, and usual composure of mind for some weeks after their admission. The following is the performance enacted on the reception of members into the Wool-combers' Union. The reader will find in it much to disgust, and something to laugh at; but whatever may be his opinion respecting it, he cannot but allow that it is well calculated to impress with feelings of awe the imaginations of the ignorant workmen, who have to undergo the ceremony. There is reason to believe that forms, very similar, if not identical to those which are detailed below, are practised by the Unions of many other trades in various parts of England. A short time back the magistrates at Exeter made a forcible entry into an apartment in that city, where the rites of a Builder s Union were proceeding, when men were discovered with their eyes bandaged, and also a skeleton, sword, battle-axe, and all the other paraphernalia, exactly as described in the following scene. A London journeyman, who entered a Union during the past year, was so overcome by the ceremonies he went through on his admission, that he was literally deprived of reason, and died in the agonies of raving madness.

DRAMATIS PERSONÆ.

Outside Tiler*—*a member of the Union who keeps guard on the outside of the room in which the members are assembled.*

Inside Tiler—*ditto on the inside.*

Principal Conductor—*the person who conducts to the Lodge those who are to be initiated into the mysteries of the Union.*

President.

Vice-President.

Warden.

Secretary.

Members of the Union.

Workmen about to be made members.

The scene is usually the first floor of a tavern, which is doubly planked throughout, and the interstices filled with wood shavings, in order to prevent any one overhearing the ceremonies. The time is 8 or 9 o'clock in the evening, at which hour the above-named dramatis personæ, with the exception of the principal conductor, and those who are about to enter the Union, are supposed to be collected together for the performance of the following drama. On one side of the apartment is a skeleton, above which is a drawn sword and a battle-axe, and in front stands a table, upon which lies a Bible. The principal officers of the Union are clothed in surplices.

---

* " Tiler" is technically a Masonic term, which originated in the circumstance, that on the first establishment of Freemasonry, those who were employed to guard the door, were really the working tilers, who had joined the confederacy.

(Members say the following prayer.)

O God, who art the author of peace and lover of concord, defend us in this our undertaking, that we may not fear the power of our adversaries, through the merits of Jesus Christ our Lord. *Amen.*

(Outside Tiler knocks at the door.)

Inside Tiler.

Who comes here to disturb the peace and harmony of this our most worthy and honourable order ?

Principal Conductor from without.

I am not come here to disturb the peace and harmony of this your most worthy and honourable order. I am a brother with strangers, who wish to be admitted into your most worthy and honourable order.

Inside Tiler.

Most worthy President, Vice, Secretary, and brothers all, a brother stands at the door with strangers, who wish to be admitted into this your most worthy and honourable order.

President.

In the name of the Lord admit him.

(Enter Principal Conductor, followed by the strangers with their eyes bandaged. Members salute, and then sing a hymn.)

Principal Conductor.

Strangers, within our secret walls we have admitted you,
Hoping you will prove honest, faithful, just and true,
If you cannot keep the secrets we require,
Go hence, you are at liberty to retire.
Are your motives pure ?

Strangers.

Yes.

Principal Conductor.

Do you declare they are?

Strangers.

Yes.

Principal Conductor.

Then, brethren, to initiate these strangers we will now proceed,
And our most worthy master may proceed to read.

(*Members sing a hymn.*)

Warden.

Stand, ye presumptuous mortals, strangers' steps I hear,
And I must know your trade and business here.
By my great power, there's nothing can from vengeance stay us,
If you come here intending to betray us.

President.

Most worthy guardian of our sacred laws,
They are wool-combers, and wishful to protect the united cause.

Warden.

Then all is well.

Vice-President.

Strangers, you are welcome, and if you prove sincere,
You'll not repent your pains and labour here.
We have one common interest, and one common soul,
Which should by virtue guide and actuate the whole.
Our trade requires protection, by experience sad we know;
Our duty is to prevent recurrence of our former woe.
Our commonwealth was like some savage land,
Where the weak are slaves, and strongest bear command,
Where tyrants rule with uncontrolled sway,
And degraded subjects do their will obey.
Such was our domestic lot. Our suffering and our care
Enraged our minds with sadness and despair.

And when we had united and our rights obtained,
We found that only half our point was gained,
Our interests were so many and so various,
The tenure of our rights so frail and so precarious,
That had we not invented Lodges our protection to ensure,
All, all would have come to nought, as it had done before.
Strangers, the design of all our Lodges is love and unity,
With self-protection founded on the laws of equity,
And when you have our mystic rights gone through,
Our secrets all will be disclosed to you.
We deem you worthy our friendship, trust and confidence to share,
See that you make the prosperity of our cause your constant care.
Let your tongue be always faithful, your heart conceal its trust,
Woe, woe and dishonour attend the faithless and unjust.
Guards, give the strangers sight.

(The bandages are removed from the eyes of the strangers, and they are placed opposite the skeleton.)

President, *pointing to the skeleton.*

Strangers, mark well this shadow, which you see,
It is a faithful emblem of man's destiny.
Behold that head once filled with pregnant wit,
These hollow holes once sparkling eyes did fit ;
This empty mouth nor lips nor tongue contains,
Of a once well furnished head, see all that now remains,
Behold this breast, where a generous heart once moved,
Filled with affection, loving and beloved,
Mark well these bones, the flesh hath left its place ;
These arms could once a tender wife embrace.
Those legs in gay activity could roam,
But, alas ! the spirit's dead, the life is gone.
O death ! O death ! thy terrors strike us with dismay,
Only the spirit just, which hath left its empty clay,
Can set thee at defiance and in triumph say,
O death, where is thy sting ? O grave, where is thy victory ?
The sting of death is sin—are we not sinners all ?
Then upon us one day the heavy stroke of death must fall.

Vice-President.

Strangers, hear me ; and mark well what I say,
Be faithful to your trust, or you may rue this day.

You are now within our secret walls, and I must know if you can keep a secret.

Strangers.

Yes.

Vice-President.
And will you do ?

Strangers.

Yes.

Vice-President.

Then amongst us, you will shortly be entitled to the endearing name
of brother,
And what you hear or see here done, you must not disclose to any
other ;
We are uniting to cultivate friendship, as well as to protect our
trade,
And due respect must to all our laws be paid.
Hoping you will prove faithful, and all encroachments on our rights
withstand,
As a token of your alliance,—give me your hand.

And now, shouldst thou ever prove deceitful, remember thy end,
remember. Guards, put these strangers into darkness, and conduct
them to our most worthy master, to be further instructed in this our
most worthy and honourable order.

> (*The eyes of the strangers are again bandaged, and they
> are then made to walk several times round the room,
> while the members stamp on the floor with their feet.
> They are then led to the table, upon which the Bible
> is placed; the right hand of each is laid upon the
> sacred volume, the bandages are then removed from
> their eyes, and they take the following oath ;*)—

I, A. B., woolcomber, being in the awful presence of Almighty
God, do voluntarily declare that I will persevere in endeavouring to

support a brotherhood, known by the name of the Friendly Society of Operative Stuff Manufacturers, and other Industrious Operatives, and I solemnly declare and promise that I will never act in opposition to the brotherhood in any of their attempts to support wages, but will, to the utmost of my power, assist them in all lawful and just occasions, to obtain a fair remuneration for our labour. And I call upon God to witness this my most solemn declaration, that neither hopes, fears, rewards, punishments, nor even death itself, shall ever induce me directly or indirectly, to give any information respecting any thing contained in this Lodge, or any similar Lodge connected with the Society; and I will neither write, nor cause to be written, upon paper, wood, sand, stone, or any thing else, whereby it may be known, unless allowed to do so by the proper authorities of the Society. And I will never give my consent to have any money belonging to the Society divided or appropriated to any other purpose than the use of the Society and support of the trade, so help me God, and keep me steadfast in this my most solemn obligation; and if ever I reveal either part or parts of this my most solemn obligation, may all the Society I am about to belong to, and all that is just, disgrace me so long as I live; and may what is now before me plunge my soul into the everlasting pit of misery. Amen.

Vice-President.

Guards, put these strangers into darkness. Rise and stand (*to the strangers*).

> (*The strangers having been blindfolded, the members sing a hymn, and then salute. The strangers are then led out. Members then say the following prayer:*)—

O God, who art the author of peace, &c. (*same as at the commencement.*)

President.

In the name of King Edward the Third,* I declare this Lodge to be now duly closed, and so it is.

---

* In this king's reign the woollen manufacture was introduced into England.

God save our noble King,
William the Fourth let's sing,
Brethren, ere we depart, let us join hand and heart
In this our cause ;
May our next meeting be blest with sweet harmony,
Honour, and secrecy in the Mechanic's cause.   [*Exeunt*

Blasphemous and horrible as is the oath above given, there is reason to believe that it was still more strongly worded, till about a year ago. In December, 1832, a murder was committed in the neighbourhood of Leeds, on a man who had refused to join in a turn-out, that had been ordered by the Clothiers' Union. In the commission of this crime, the members of the Union were strongly implicated, and on the inquest that was held on the body, a witness, who had once belonged to the Union, the father of the murdered man, gave an account of the mode of making members. His statement of the ceremonial tallies pretty nearly with that which has been given, but being an illiterate man, and having to trust to his memory alone, his testimony is meagerly and confusedly given. From what can be collected from the evidence of this witness, it is obvious, that the oath which he took, included a more dreadful imprecation on the head of the taker, should he violate it, than that above given. The publication of this evidence naturally excited in the public mind considerable disgust against the Union, and in the next grand meeting, held six weeks afterwards, we find, by a book of their proceedings, that a resolution was passed, substituting the oath that has been presented to the reader for the one previously used. There is, therefore, reason to suspect, that owing to this murder, and the circumstances that arose from it, the terms of the oath were considerably softened, with the view of preventing the Union suffering so much in public estimation, should the actual words ever be known. What were the words before the alteration can only be conjectured, but the oath contained in the above ceremonial is so nearly identical with one used by a political society at Glasgow, in 1817, that probably the Scotch oath was taken entire. If this supposition be correct, the Yorkshire oath, before the murder, must have contained a clause, by which the taker of it invoked on himself, should he prove false, "the punishment of death to be inflicted on him by any member or members of the Society."

The following is the oath that was taken by the combined spinners in Scotland in 1823, whether it is the same as is taken now we are not aware. "I, A. B., do voluntarily swear, in the awful presence of Almighty God, and before these witnesses, that I will execute, with zeal and alacrity, as far as in me lies, every task or injunction, which the majority of my brethren shall impose upon me in furtherance of our common welfare; as the chastisement of knobs, the assassination of oppressive and tyrannical masters, or the demolition of shops that shall be deemed incorrigible; and also that I will cheerfully contribute to the support of my brethren

as shall lose their work in consequence of their
exertions against tyranny, or renounce it in resistance to a reduction of wages; and I do further
swear, that I will never divulge the above obligation, unless I shall have been duly authorized and
appointed to administer the same to persons making
application for admission, or to persons constrained
to become members of our fraternity."

This oath is perhaps the most atrocious that has
ever been put. It recognises the principle of compelling persons to enter the Union, and openly
sanctions assaults and murder. We are not aware
whether it has ever been used by the English
Unions, but the religious feelings of those who
have joined them in this country, must sometimes
have been at least as much shocked by the excessive blasphemy that characterises their proceedings. For instance, the reading of the 94th Psalm
sometimes forms part of the ceremonies of admission; a Psalm, of which the title is *Deus ultionum*,
and which calls in the strongest language for the
infliction of the Almighty vengeance on transgres-
sors, that is, in this case, the employers.

Combinations in England, though they have
been fertile in assaults and outrages of various
kinds, have rarely led to murder. The only crime
of this sort that can be laid to the charge of the
Yorkshire Union, is that which took place at Farsly,
a small village in the neighbourhood of Leeds, in
December, 1832. The murdered man had become
obnoxious to the Union, by refusing to join in a

strike ; and though the charge could not be proved
against the members, the circumstances told so
strongly against them, that the jury which sat on
the inquest, gave in their verdict, that they had
" too much reason to fear, that his murder had
been the consequence of fidelity to his master !"
The night of the murder, the Union had had a long
and violent discussion, which lasted from six to
eleven ; at half-past eight the object of their hatred
was attacked in a lane by between thirty and forty
persons, and beaten to death with clubs. Not one
of these ruffians ever made a sign of their guilt,
and the perpetrators are still undiscovered. In
the course of three years, ten lives were lost in
Dublin in consequence of combinations, and in
no one instance were the murderers brought to
justice.

There appears no reason to doubt, and it would
be an object of national utility, could the truth be
impressed on the minds of the workmen, that their
combinations have not succeeded in raising, but,
on the contrary, have sometimes caused a depres-
sion of wages. Instances of the mode in which
their object has been baffled, have been given from
the cotton trade ; but it may be of advantage to
add some examples from other trades, in order to
shew the universality of the obstacles that oppose
the attainment of their wishes. Many of the Leeds
workmen themselves allow, that they have gained
nothing by entering into a combination, the contributions necessary to support which, cause a

never-ceasing drain on their pockets. One case has been mentioned, in which the Union spent 4000*l.* in a fruitless attempt to bring a master under their control, the only result of which was to cause many new workmen to enter the trade, and thus lower the rate of their wages. The shipwrights in Liverpool struck for an advance of wages in 1816, and having continued idle twenty-two weeks, returned to their work at five per cent. reduction from what they were receiving when they turned out. The hatters in London struck in 1820, demanding an increase of 1*s.* per dozen hats ; and after staying out for fifteen weeks, they accepted employment from their masters at a *decrease* of 1*s.* instead of a rise of that sum, which they had forfeited nearly a third of a year's wages to gain.

Where the workmen have succeeded in compelling their employers to raise wages, they have equally failed to derive benefit, or even to escape injury from the change, though it is of course more difficult in this case to trace the means by which this effect has been produced. It has either arisen from the high wages attracting more labourers to enter the trade in which they have been given, than can be supplied with work, and who consequently must be supported by those who get work, else the competition of their numbers will beat down the advance that has been obtained ; in both which cases the advance, or more than the advance, is instantly lost ; or it has arisen from the expense of maintaining the various burdens which a combination entails, such as clerks, secretaries, delegates, meeting-rooms, &c.—from the falling off of consumption in consequence of the increase of price; and therefore less being manufactured, and less wages distributed among the body of the Unionists,—from the driving away of the manufacture to other places,—from some one of these or other causes, the advantage vanishes in the moment of expected fruition, and generally leaves the workmen in a worse state than before. On this point, some valuable evidence was taken by the Committee of the House of Commons, that sat last Session, to inquire into the state of trade. Mr. Jackson, a manufacturer at Sheffield, where the combinations have done almost irreparable injury to the cutlery business, says, on his examination:—

" The workman does not benefit, strictly speaking, by combination; though he gets high wages, he has sometimes to pay 20 per cent. out of his wages for keeping up the combination, besides an occasional levy of 1 *l.*! and besides, to obtain this advantage, it frequently happens that they are out of employment for several months, so that I have frequently said to the workmen, that I defy them to prove that any steady industrious man ever benefited by it; that is to say, that the cost of obtaining the advance is greater than the advantage ultimately realized.—Have the combinations you have mentioned had the tendency of raising the price generally?—My opinion is, that they have a tendency ultimately to reduce it; an augmentation of wages has taken place; if trade has been remarkably brisk, and the demand made by the workmen has mostly been for an exorbitant price, this price has generally been maintained for a very short time, for a month, perhaps, to execute the orders on hand, but the price of goods was in consequence so far augmented, as to stop the demand in our foreign markets, and a subsequent reaction taking place, it has been ascertained, that after a turn-out of workmen, and a consequent augmentation in the price of goods, every third season, or every third half-year, (as the American orders come usually twice a year), the price has fallen much below the previous level ; and when workmen have attempted to gain exorbitant wages for their labour, it has ended in the sequel, by bringing the rate of their labour to a less standard than that from which they previously started.

Another witness, John Milner, gives the following evidence on this point. He was a journeyman till within the last three years, and was deputed by the Freeman's Society, which is composed principally of journeymen, to attend the Committee :—

Is it your opinion, that those combinations have been successful in effecting their objects, and in amending the condition of the workmen ?—They have been unsuccessful generally.

What have been their effects ? have they had any effect in increasing or diminishing the fluctuation of wages ?—They have in general failed in their object ; indeed, I may say on almost every occasion, they have ultimately failed ; they have seldom had a tendency to establish any regular wages.

During the time of those combinations, have not the contributions of the workmen cost them as much as they have gained by the keeping up their wages ?—In many instances, the loss of time, and the expense, has been much more than the benefit resulting from it during the time that it existed. I believe that in Sheffield, the rage for combination begins to subside, and many of the workmen, who were zealous advocates for combinations a few years since, have had the combination surfeit.

Numerous instances may be quoted of manufactures being driven from the places in which they were originally established, owing to the combinations of the workmen engaged in them. Both Paisley and Macclesfield owe their rise to the high wages demanded in Spitalfields; and Macclesfield in turn has lost part of its silk trade to the benefit of Manchester, from the same causes that had before driven it from London. Some manufacturers have lately left Coventry, owing to the continual annoyances from strikes to which they were exposed in that town, and established factories in Essex. The combination at Leeds have thrown many of the looms idle in that town, to the profit of the weavers in the neighbouring villages, and more especially of the clothing establishments in the West of England, whither many orders for goods have been sent during the last summer, owing to the difficulty of executing them in Yorkshire. The carpet trade has been seriously injured by the strikes in Kidderminster, and has in consequence partly migrated to Kilmarnock. But perhaps Ireland has suffered more than any other country in this way by the folly of its working population. Owing to the Union in Dublin, planks can be cut into boards thirty-five per cent. cheaper in Liverpool than in that town; and, consequently, shipbuilding, which has been long lingering in Ireland, although the demand for all kinds of vessels is rapidly on the increase, threatens speedily to desert the shores of that island altogether. Some time ago, an Irish manufacturer required for his business several large metal utensils, and being desirous that his own country should have the profit of supplying them, he called upon the master of some iron-works, and stated his readiness to sacrifice a considerable per-centage, rather than that the order should be sent out of the country. The master informed him that he was incapacitated from manufacturing the articles, even at the proposed advance of price, and that he was prevented from competing with his English rivals, not from any want of coal, or from any local advantages that were possessed on the other side of the Channel, but solely on account of the combinations by which he was beset. The result was, that the manufacturer was obliged to have recourse to the English market.* Mr. Robinson, an extensive iron-master in Dublin, constructed, several years ago, a machine for the manufacture of nails; the nail-makers determined to prevent its use, and got the workmen in those trades in which nails are used, to pass a resolution, that they would not work with any that had been made by this machine. Consequently, machine-made nails from Birmingham quickly drove the Dublin ones out of the market; the manufacture of nails left the latter place altogether, and has, we believe, never returned. Dr. Doyle, in his evidence before the Irish Committee of 1830, gives some remarkable instances of the evil his country has sustained from combinations. He is asked,

Do you not think it a desirable object to illustrate to the labouring classes, and particularly to artizans, the evil effects of

* Dublin Evening Post, Dec. 19th, 1833.

G

those combinations, which have so much retarded and checked industry in Ireland ?—If artizans particularly could be so convinced, very great advantages would result both to themselves and to the community at large, for their combinations are most injurious to the public interest. The week before I left home, I spent a few days in Kilkenny, on a visit with the Catholic Bishop of Ossory. They were at that time disposing in that city of a fund of 300*l.* or 400*l.* raised for the relief of the poor. There was a question of setting to work the unemployed weavers, which led to my inquiry into some particulars with regard to them. It was the opinion, however, of those gentlemen, then conversing, that the combinations among that description of work-people were the chief cause of the almost extinction of the blanket manufacture in Kilkenny, and though the citizens were then obliged to relieve them out of the public funds, these weavers themselves were the cause of their own misfortunes ; for as soon as they discovered that a manufacturer had a contract for making blankets, or that there was a demand for goods, they immediately struck, and would not work unless for very high prices : hence the manufacturers were unable to enter into contracts, lest they should be disappointed, or that too high wages would be extorted from them ; and the consequence was that the manufacture went down altogether.

Do you consider those combinations amongst the artizans and manufacturers one of the most serious difficulties to the extension of manufacturing industry in Ireland ?—It is one of the great obstacles to it.

A Dublin witness also stated before the Combination Committee of 1825, that he knew " five persons in different branches, and all largely connected in trade, not one of whom would take a contract, from the conviction, that the moment it was known they had taken a contract, there would be a strike among their men."

At the present time, the trade of the Irish capital seems in great measure paralysed by the Unions, and outrages to forward their objects are of frequent occurrence. These facts, perhaps, afford at least as probable a solution of the causes that have depressed Irish industry, and that of Dublin in particular, which has been so eminently distinguished by its spirit of combination, as any others that have been brought forward.

But an evil of far more serious import to the nation, is, when the manufacture, instead of changing from one part of the country to another, leaves it altogether, and takes refuge in foreign parts. This has actually been done in some instances, and the rapid increase of Continental rivalry, by disseminating more widely, habits and models of manufacturing industry, daily renders such migration of easier execution. It is obvious, indeed, that if this effect has not more generally followed, every additional attack on the profits of the home manufacturer must have this tendency, and augment the chances of foreign products successfully competing with British.

One case has been mentioned, in which a cotton manufacturer established a factory at New York, that he might conduct his business free from those interruptions, to which it was subjected in this country from the strikes among his men. The conduct of the Sheffield workmen already threatens the extinction of the trade of that town, and its transference to our French and German rivals. At present the same labour in the manufacture of saws which costs 15s. or 20s. at Sheffield, can be

done for 1*s*. 3*d*. at Molsheim, in the neighbourhood of Strasburg. The consequence is, the ex-
portation of this article to the Continent, which was
considerable some years ago, has almost wholly
ceased, many other of the Sheffield productions
have shared the same fate, and America is almost
the only market that is left for the sale of the manufactures of that town. At present the condition of the Sheffield operatives is far worse in
respect of comfort, than at any preceding period,
and the town exhibits the extraordinary spectacle,
the inevitable result of successful combinations, of
high wages, a decaying trade, and a destitute population. The business that remains is now dependent on our friendly relations with the United
States ; war, or the policy of a tariff may equally
extinguish it, and should that happen, the Sheffield workmen may perhaps at length learn, amidst
unavailing regrets, that the question has not been,
whether they shall get high or moderate wages, but
the latter or none at all.

An instance of transference of a manufacture to
the Continent, in consequence of strikes, has lately
occurred in the woollen trade. The workmen in
a large cloth-dying establishment in Yorkshire
turned-out for an advance of wages. It happened
that the firm were large exporters of *finished* cloth
to Germany, where they possessed a small dying
factory, of which, however, little use was made.
The proprietors, on the stoppage of their business
in England, were induced to try the experiment of

sending the greater part of their cloth in a white state to Germany, and dying it there, where they could be free from the dictation of Trades' Unions. The experiment not only answered expectation, but many other unlooked-for advantages resulted from the change. A saving was made in the expense of insurance, as the article was less valuable when in course of transit; there was also less risk of its being spoilt by sea-water, as the subsequent dying remedied any damage it might sustain from this cause. Consequently, the proprietors in question have been transferring their dying business to Germany, carrying their skill and experience with them; large additions have been made to their foreign factory, and whereas, before the strike, they did not export above 500 pieces of undyed cloth weekly, they now send from 1000 to 1200 in the same time. As increased profit has attended this change in the locality of their dying trade, it is clear that this firm will never bring back its business to England, on the contrary, it is to be feared, that the example will be imitated by other firms, and the eventual result may be, that the profit of dying all the cloth that is sent to Germany, amounting to nearly 20,000 pieces annually, may be lost to this country.*

---

* Since the above was written, the author has had reason to doubt, whether the circumstances of the case are stated with perfect accuracy. That the dying business of the firm has been transferred, as related, is certain; but the proprietors may have been actuated by other reasons, than those above given. Where a mixture of motives

It may be asked, how it was, that the manufacturer did not discover the most profitable mode of carrying on his business before the strike. The answer is, that his attention was not turned to this particular point. It might as well be asked why the wool-combing machine was not invented ten years ago instead of now, or why the French did not make sugar from beet-root before Napoleon's time, as well as after, since these inventions were equally possible, and would have been as profitable then as at present. People do not forsake, what has become habitual to them, without the excitement of some external cause; new and improved modes of carrying on trades are constantly discovered, as obstacles impede their ancient course, and necessity sharpens invention.

Two curious facts are established with the utmost certainty by a consideration of the history of turn-outs. First, that they are hardly ever resorted to, except by those, who habitually receive high wages, and secondly, that the time of their occurrence is almost invariably when trade is prosperous. In cotton-spinning mills, strikes are nearly unknown except amongst the spinners, and

has prompted any conduct, it is difficult to assign its due weight to each, but among those, which have brought about the change in question, must be enumerated the high duty on drugs in England, and the low one on the importation of undyed as compared with dyed cloth into Germany. The evil, however, is equally well shewn, in *possibility*, according to the alleged example, as it would be in *reality*, by the fact.

they earn far higher wages, with the exception of the overlookers, than any other persons in a factory, indeed more than double what is got by the majority. When the fine spinners in Manchester turned-out in 1829, to the number of 1000, they refused work, by which they could earn from 30s. to 35s. clear per week. When 52 mills, and 30,000 persons were thrown idle during ten weeks in 1830, at Ashton and the neighbourhood, by the turning-out of 3000 coarse spinners, these men could earn weekly from 28s. to 31s. clear. In the woollen trade, the weavers, and in the worsted, the combers, both of whom get from 16s. to 20s. weekly, are the usual ringleaders in strikes. Evidence from various quarters in proof of this position is given in the note below,* and also respecting the

* Mr. Dunlop examined. Combination Committee, 1824.

" What was the rate of wages you gave during this time, when this combination took place ?—The machinery I now have in that mill is calculated for women, it is now worked by men, and they get 30s. a week, clear of all charges.

What was the rate of wages paid in that mill, at the time the combinations took place for an advance of wages ?—Above 30s.

Was the trade brisk at that time ?—Very good, they never turn-out when the trade is bad.

There are no turns-out when trade is bad ?—No."

Mr. Jones examined. Combination Committee, 1824.

" According to your experience, it was when wages have been high, that the combinations have taken place, and not when they were low ?—Yes, it has been when they (spinners) have got most, that they have turned out."

Mr. Jackson examined, Committee of Manufactures and Commerce, 1833.

coincidence of strikes with a briskness of trade. It is not difficult to understand the reason of this latter result. There is greater likelihood of a master yielding to the wishes of his men, when he

---

" In times of good trade they (combinations in Sheffield) have been sustained; in bad trade they have been broken up or provisionally suspended.—Some of these combinations have lasted without intermission since 1810, but others have been broken up every returning period of bad trade ; but as soon as trade becomes better, the combinations spring up afresh."

Mr. Hebblethwaite examined. Combination Committee, 1825.

" About two years ago we took an order for some ladies cloths ; we were to complete them in six weeks ; as soon as we got the order we were obliged to tell the men we should want them completed in six weeks ; when we did that the men turned out immediately.— Those that have the most wages are the worst people to deal with ; those that we give most money to, have been our biggest enemies."

Mr. Bowler examined. Combination Committee, 1824.

" They (journeymen hatters) take care to turn-out in the spring of the year, and that is the time, when every master wants his journeymen, and of course his trade is standing still ; his customers want to be supplied with hats."

Mr. Farrel examined. Combination Committee, 1825.

" In point of fact has not the plenty of work, and the consequent supply of money that the persons in work have had, enabled them to combine to support their brethren out of work ?—Yes.

Is not work, in general, very brisk in Dublin ?—Every sort of work is brisk in Dublin.

Does not that afford them facilities for combining for raising their wages ?—It does, and always did.

Have you found that when the men were in demand, combinations for rise of wages were most frequent ?—Yes; that is one of the greatest misfortunes a master has to encounter ; he makes his contract, and the moment he does that, the men turn-out for rise of wages."

has many orders on hand, than when he works on speculation. In the former case, non-compliance may benefit his rivals in trade, and he is better able to comply, as prices are always higher ; in the latter, his profit being precarious, a stoppage of his works may be less hurtful to him. Besides, it is only when work is abundant, that those who strike can depend on being supported by their brethren who remain employed ; at other times, the weekly subscriptions are so irregularly paid, that the funds of the combination are wholly insufficient to maintain its idle members. It is not here intended to assert, that strikes always accompany a prosperous trade, but that their existence in any business affords a strong presumption, approaching to certainty, that it is in a thriving condition. It has been much discussed in the past year, whether our manufactures were in a flourishing or decaying state during that time. We should at once decide by reference to the foregoing reasons. They *have* been flourishing beyond all precedent, because combinations have never been so rife, nor strikes so frequent. An exception to this remark must be made with respect to the cotton-spinning trade, which has been undisturbed by strikes, though the Spinners' Union, the most powerful in England, exists in it. The exception proves our rule, for this business has not been flourishing during the last year, and the Manchester factories have only worked eight hours daily. Wages for a time were reduced a third, and the combinations were unheard of.

It has been supposed that these Societies have some connection with the political circumstances of the times. Their present vigour has been attributed to the Reform Bill, to the French Revolution, to an hostility to the Established Church, to a spread of democratical principles, and other causes of a like nature. There does not appear to be the smallest ground for these opinions. Their whole object has been to raise wages, and to this point alone all their energies have been directed. With many, a principle of their constitution is to abstain from all interference in religion and politics ; and to this, they have all, as far as we are aware, studiously adhered, unless indeed, the interest which some of them took in the Factory Bill, though even here the secret object was to raise wages, be considered an exception to this remark. Among some " observations and cautions" appended to the rules of one of the most extensive Unions in Yorkshire, are the following :—" Brethren, you are cautiously to avoid all religious disputes, as quarrels from this source have ever been found prejudicial, and often destructive to society ; let every brother freely enjoy his own opinion, but not lord it over another, nor introduce any particular intricate wranglings in the Lodge. Political disputes having an equal tendency to inflame the passions and sour the temper, are therefore with equal propriety excluded from our Lodges ; you are enjoined to pay a due obedience to the laws, and respect to the Government of our country, and to live as peaceable subjects, but never to disturb or embroil the Lodge with your particular opinion of state affairs." By a rule of the Union of the Seamen of the Tyne and Wear, a fine of 5*s.* was imposed on any member, who should " speak contemptuously of the present King and Constitution ;" and the regulations of the Coal-miners' combination given in the Appendix, enact, " that if any member speak disrespectfully of the State and laws of the nation, his Majesty, or either of the Houses of Parliament, or any magistrate, he shall forfeit 2*s.* 6*d.* for every such offence." But were they not actuated by these feelings, it is not likely that they would ever assume any strong political character, so long as the law on this subject remains in its present state, since such a change would instantly render them liable to the severe penalties of the 57 Geo. III. c. 19.

A curious circumstance occurred with respect to the religious feelings of some members of the Spinners' Union, when the national delegates of that association met in the Isle of Man in 1829. It happened that the assembly held its first meeting on a Saturday, when the Scotch members proposed that no business whatever should be transacted the next day, and moved, that the meeting, on its rising, should adjourn to the ensuing Monday. The English delegates were opposed to this plan, as involving a loss of time, besides an increase of expense. But the Scotchmen, with the characteristic pertinacity of their nation on such points, argued so warmly in its favour,—protesting that, if their constituents knew that the Sabbath would be devoted to business, they would consider that no good could attend the Union, and would positively refuse to support it,—that they finally carried their motion. This fact forms a curious comment on the atrocious violence by which, in Scotland, above all other places, the proceedings of this Union have been marked. The rigid austerity with which Sunday is every where observed in the North, leads to the conclusion, that the countrymen of Knox were not misrepresented on this occasion. But do they inconsistently suppose that the end will sometimes sanctify the means? At any events, it stands as a psychological curiosity, that men, who do not hesitate to put and take oaths binding to murder, and to act with a ferocity proportionate to such conduct, can consider it a pollution of the Sabbath, to discuss on that day what concerns (in their opinion) the saving of themselves and families from "poverty, degradation, and crime."*

One of the worst features of these Societies, is their hostility to piece or task-work, and the consequent discouragement they give to the exercise of superior skill and industry. "The man who does task-work," says the Trades' Union Magazine,—"is guilty of less defensible conduct than a drunkard. The worst passions of our nature are enlisted in support of task-work. Avarice,

* Speech of one of the delegates, respecting the objects of their Association, delivered at the meeting alluded to.

meanness, cunning, hypocrisy, all excite and feed upon the miserable victim of task-work, while debility and destitution look out for the last morsel of their prey. A man, who earns by task-work, 40s. per week, the usual wages by day being 20s., robs his fellow of a week's employment." The discouragement of merit, is, indeed, the necessary consequence of the attempt to establish what is called " an equalization of wages," a state of things, in which every one is to earn an equal sum, without reference to his talent or diligence. To this desire is owing the absurd rule in the Appendix, which imposes the penalty of 2s. 6d. or expulsion from the Society, on any member, who should " be known to boast of his superior ability as to either the quantity or quality of work he can do, either in public or private company." An universal enthusiasm for the good of our species is to produce that skill, which is now the effect of rivalry, and, in conformity with the doctrines of Owen and the St. Simonians, which these Societies have either copied or originated, emulation is to be chased from the world, as the source of all evil. But it must be confessed, that the benevolence inculcated by the teachers in this science, is a little scandalized in the practice of the pupils. One of the foulest murders that has ever disgraced Dublin, was perpetrated on a man, whose only crime was a desire to gain those wages to which he was justly entitled by superior skill. Perhaps, according to this code, the diffusion of its principles and influence, consequent on the crime, justified the commission of it. The terror inspired by the deed, caused almost all the neighbouring workmen to join the Union, and Dublin advanced one step onwards towards the reign of universal peace and love!

These Unions, when their rules are strictly followed, produce similar results, though in a more aggravated shape, to those which arise from a poor-rate, and labour-rate, in their worst forms of abuse. If a workman throw himself out of employ, because he is not satisfied with his wages, a weekly payment of 8s. or 10s. is ready for his acceptance, which he can demand as his right, and enjoy in idleness. He can gain nothing by superior qualifications for his business, and lose nothing by the want of them; industry will not increase his wages, or negligence depress them, but the earnings of all are reduced to one common level, an attempt to raise which, by any one man, is treated as an offence to the general body.

Another inducement to idleness is held out to members of combinations, equally forcible with that, which arises from the interdiction of piece-work, and beyond what could be produced by any poor-law. The constant and heavy drains which the subscriptions to their Unions make on the wages of the workmen, naturally create a strong desire to get some immediate return for the outlay. The advance of wages, which they may happen to get, is seldom, as has been shewn above, even apparently beneficial to them, the loss of this advance following almost instantaneously its receipt. But idleness, with ten or twelve shillings a week, is the alternative to continuing at work ; and this, as has been frequently proved in the operation of the poor-laws, is preferred by many to double that sum received as the reward of labour. The Unionist has an additional reason for such a preference, as it is more clearly his right, and he only receives back his own money. Hence, though a desire to raise wages, or prevent their reduction, is always the professed reason of a turn-out, the workmen are often fully aware of the impossibility of complying with their demands, and the wish to live for a time in idleness, is the latent motive of their conduct. He who strikes in the first instance to change low wages into high, may thus commit the inconsistency of a second strike, to change high wages into a low pittance without labour. It is true, that such an employment of the funds, must counteract the main object with which they are contributed, by lessening, or wholly annihilating the power of turning-out, when, in the opinion of the men, such a step may be expedient. But the ignorant are ever improvident; with such persons, present enjoyment, however small, is frequently preferred to future, however great; and the more intelligent leaders of the Unions often lament, while they confess the impossibility of controlling, the hasty and inconsiderate conduct of the members.

One of the worst results of combinations, is the

delusion, which they sanction, that wages are not subject to the general laws of demand and supply, but are dependent on the pleasure of the employers. Wages, say the Unionists, would be beaten down by the masters, to the lowest amount that could suffice for a maintenance, were it not for the combinations. But the earnings of men, who have never joined the Unions, have not been so beaten down. Combinations and strikes are unknown among the overlookers in cotton factories, and yet they are paid more than any other persons in such establishments. Nine-tenths of the cotton-workers never think of forming Unions, and the alleged advantage has never been taken of them by their masters. The wages of the throstle-spinners, for instance, have hardly varied for thirty years, and are, consequently, now, if measured in clothes and provisions, at least 30 per cent. higher, than they used to be. Have the mule-spinners, on the other hand, gained more by their combinations and strikes? Amidst the nearly universal prevalence of this absurd error, it is cheering to find an instance in Glasgow, of the recognition by the workmen of the principle, that the number of labourers is one of the chief elements in settling the price of labour. By the evidence of a large Glasgow manufacturer, given before a Parliamentary Committee last Session, it appears, that the spinners in that town have applied part of their funds towards paying the emigration expenses of some of their class, and in this way have got rid of one-eighth of their numbers.

In those places where combinations have been most frequent and powerful, a complete separation of feeling seems to have taken place between masters and men. Each party looks on the other as an enemy, and suspicion and distrust have driven out the mutual sentiments of kindness and good-will, by which their intercourse was previously marked. A dispute between them is settled by no joint understanding; the two sides are not even allowed to discuss the matter, but reference must be made to a junta, chosen by the workmen alone. Thus shackled in his operations, a master must either refuse all large orders for goods, or take them under the trembling apprehension, that should it so please the Union, his profit may be taken away, or even a loss incurred by the undertaking. In some establishments, a large quantity of the article, ready for sale, is always kept on hand, in order to insure the proprietors against the losses occasioned by strikes. In one case, coal to the value of 10,000l. was constantly laid by to meet this exigence, and such an addition to the fixed capital employed in the mine, must of course have increased the cost of working it, and the price of the coal when obtained; consequently, the consumption of the article, and the demand for workmen in this line of business, must have been lessened.* A suppression of speculation is an obvious result of these interferences with the transactions of the manufacturers; and, in fact, the

* Babbage's Economy of Manufactures, 283.

workmen in some places, with suicidal folly almost
inconceivable, have proclaimed their hostility to
speculation in their employers. The members of
a combination in the Staffordshire Potteries, actually passed a resolution, that the masters should
only employ their men, on receiving orders for
goods, and never in anticipation of a demand.
Where a large capital is invested in machinery
and buildings, the workmen are enabled to exercise a much greater control over their employers,
as the simple stoppage of the works inflicts a serious loss on the proprietors. It is not at all an unusual circumstance for 80,000*l.* to be invested in a
cotton-mill; the interest of this capital exceeds
75*l.* weekly, consequently that sum must be lost
to the possessors of such a mill, every week that
the men hold out.

It is an impression universally entertained by the
labouring classes, and very generally by the public,
that masters are in the habit of combining for the
purpose of lowering wages. To this erroneous
opinion, as we shall endeavour to prove it, Adam
Smith has lent the sanction of his name. " Masters,
he says, " are always and every where in a sort of
tacit, but constant and uniform combination, not
to raise the wages of labour above their actual rate.
To violate this combination is every where a most
unpopular action, and a sort of reproach to a master among his neighbours and equals. We seldom,
indeed, hear of this combination, because it is the
usual, and one may say the natural state of things,

which nobody ever hears of. Masters too sometimes enter into particular combinations to sink the wages of labour even below this rate. These are always conducted with the utmost silence and secrecy, till the moment of execution, and when the workmen yield, as they sometimes do without resistance, though severely felt by them, they are never heard of by other people." (*Wealth of Nations*, chap. vii.) What may have been the case in the time of Adam Smith we have no means of ascertaining, but certainly for a long period back, there is no reason to suppose such a state of things to have existed. In the evidence taken by the Combination Committee of 1824, there is only one instance related of a perfect combination of masters, that of the ten London type-founders, and it cannot have inflicted much injury on the workmen, since their wages were then 18s.* weekly, and had been so for a long time previous. The statements made to the Committee go to prove, not only that combinations do not exist among the masters, but that they cannot generally exist. The head police officer in Dublin, who had considerable experience in these matters, says, "there can never be a combination amongst masters in any trade in fact, for their interests are all separate, unless the journeymen get into a very disorderly state, and they meet to see what can be done with them ; but the masters in all trades are, in general, all at variance with each other on the subject of trade."

* At present their wages average 30s. weekly.

The jealousy, with which masters, in trades of great extent especially, regard each other, is so great, we may almost call it virulent, that nothing is more difficult than to get them to enter on any combined plan of operations. Each regards his neighbour as his rival, and sometimes, as has been stated in a preceding page, the most unjustifiable and disgraceful. means have been resorted to by one manufacturer to depress and ruin another. Some cotton-spinners in Manchester and the neighbourhood, have actually at times subscribed to the Combination Fund of the workmen, in order to organize and support a strike against a rival manufacturer. An attempt was once set on foot in this way, to compel the masters in the vicinity of Manchester, to pay their workmen the same wages as were given in that town, where they always are necessarily higher than in the country ; as might be expected, the scheme was wholly unsuccessful.

In 1821 the Colonel of a regiment of dragoons gave an order for some saddles to an army accoutrement-maker at Dublin. The master saddlers in that city, on learning this circumstance, declared it was an encroachment on their trade, and incited the journeymen who were to perform the work, to turn out against their master, who was in consequence compelled to give up the contract. The saddlers, however, did not profit by their conduct, as none of them got the order, which was thus lost to Ireland altogeher.

It is only when the workmen have proceeded to

the greatest excesses, and their tyranny has become absolutely insupportable, that the masters can be induced to unite for their common protection. And then their Union is but a rope of sand, which falls to pieces on the first opening for accommodation with the men. When four years ago, all the fine spinners in Manchester turned out, the masters were brought with great difficulty to form a combined plan of defence against the men, but so sensible were they of the jealousy that existed among themselves, that for this confessed reason, they chose a gentleman engaged in a different trade for their chairman. " As for the reduction of wages being the work of combined masters, there is, perhaps, no given subject, upon which, in the important trades, it is so impracticable to produce unity of purpose. When the master spinners of Manchester, closely beset by their workmen, their mills picqueted, and their persons in danger, met to apply to Government for protection, the advice was given, which had often before been acted upon, ' Let us keep off the subject of wages, for on that we shall never agree.' "*

When the Leeds' Combination commenced its operations by causing a strike of Messrs. Gott's workmen, the other manufacturers, so far from lending any assistance, or countenancing the opposition that was made to the demands of the Union, seemed to rejoice that a rival establishment was stopped. When shortly after, other masters were

* Combinations of Trades, p. 20.

placed in similar situations, the same feeling was shewn regarding them ; and it was only when the demands of the workmen were extending to all employers, and it was obvious that none would escape, when ruin stared them in the face, and almost irreparable damage had been done to the trade, that they began to think of opposing the combination of the men by a united effort. Even then their scheme had no reference whatever to wages, but simply proposed, that each master should sign a bond, binding himself in a considerable penalty, not to employ any workmen belonging to a Trades' Union.

Varieties in the situation of manufacturing establishments oppose insurmountable obstacles to any attempt of masters to establish a uniform rate of wages. In remote country places, the expenses of conveying the raw and finished material, the machinery, and other articles required in manufacturing processes, are so great, that mills would never be erected at all, were it not for the inducement of low wages, and they can only continue to work so long as low wages are preserved. But even where no topographical differences exist, machines for performing any particular work are of such dissimilar powers, and the modes of conducting business are so various, that it is impossible but that some corresponding variation must exist in the rate of wages. In Manchester there are as many different prices paid for spinning, as there are differences in the size of mules, and those masters whose workmen earn most, get their work cheapest done, as they are in possession of the most improved machinery. But, independent of experience, reason alone would prove the difficulty of masters ever successfully combining to pay their workmen according to a fixed and uniform scale.*

In some places Benefit Societies, legally enrolled, have been made the cloak for combinations, and thus violence and intimidation have been practised by bodies, organised under the apparent sanction of the law. This is one of the most disastrous results that can be apprehended from the spirit of Union; it is turning nourishment into poison; and making, what is calculated to confer the greatest benefits on the working classes, a source of almost unmitigated evil.

A society, termed the "Friendly Boiler Makers' Society," at Manchester, instituted July, 1832, has

---

* The Masters in a large manufacturing town in the north, lately took a very effective method of suppressing a Trades' Union. It being the practice of those bodies to commence hostilities against their employers on occasion of extensive orders, when resistance is most inconvenient, a resolution was adopted by the latter to compel the breach, while the market was overstocked, and the consequences might be encountered without injury to themselves. In pursuance of this plan, they required an abandonment of the Union by all their workmen, on pain of immediate dismission. The men struck according to expectation, and the movement having been thus precipitated at a time, and, it may be added, on terms least favourable to the object of the Unionists, they will now be compelled to exhaust their means without effect, and resume work as soon as wanted. This example, if followed, would destroy combinations, but some difficulty would be experienced in cases where a large fixed capital is employed.

a preamble printed to its rules, stating, " It having
been an ancient custom for divers artists, within
the United Kingdom to form themselves into societies, for the sole purpose of assisting each other
in cases of sickness, old age, and other infirmities,
and for the burial of the dead ; under these circumstances, the members composing this Society have
agreed to raise a fund, for the purpose aforesaid,
and further agree to the following rules, drawn up
and approved by a Committee, selected for that
purpose." And yet we find amongst its rules the
following :—"That no person who is a member of this
Society shall be allowed to work in an illegal yard.
No member shall be allowed to take work, where
the same is to be used ; or to take any work by the
plate *(this excludes piece-work)*.   Any member act-
ing contrary to this article shall, for the first offence be fined 10*s*., for the second 1*l*. 1*s*., or be excluded." And this is by far the heaviest fine, inflicted by the regulations, which contain other
clauses obviously intended to control the masters.
Another body formed at Manchester, is designated
the " Benevolent Society," and in a notice pre-
fixed to the rules, by which they profess to be
governed, they say, that they " think it their duty
thus publicly to declare, that the intention of their
institution is for the purpose *only* of mutual relief
in cases of infirmity, of accidents, and for the burial
of deceased members and their wives."   Now
amongst the rules are the four following :—-

" That if any member should hire, or bind himself for more than
one week with his employer or employers, to be excluded, and shall
not be admitted again.   Any member being discharged on the refuse

of not hiring with his employer or employers, should he or they be discharged, will be entitled to the same benefit as a turn-out, for the space of three months. Any member being discharged on the Society's account, shall be entitled to, if a foreman 15s. if a follower 9s.

" That if any foreman, or follower, or dyer, or dresser, should be discharged, the next man that takes his situation must ask the same wages ; and if he goes for less, he shall be fined one pound, and the members of the shop shall be fined 5s. each for working with him ; and if this rule be attended to, the price of labour will be kept up.

" That if any man belonging to any other trade should get employment at any legal shop in the trade, or any illegal man that is not a member of the Union, in the course of any week, the members of that shop shall give notice to their employer, that they will not work any longer than that week with such characters ; and if they neglect so to do, the members of that shop shall be fined 5s. each, and not be entitled to any benefit until the said fine be paid.

" If any foreman, either dresser or dyer, work for less than 20s. per week, will not be entitled to more than a follower, either with regard as a turn-out or otherwise."

It is curious to mark, how every evil that afflicts the country is resolvable into ignorance, and how directly education offers a remedy. Could the working classes be instructed in the laws, which regulate their wages, combinations from that moment would cease to exist. They would learn that wages are not dependent on the will of those who pay them, and that they can only be altered by changing the proportion between the number of labourers and the funds set apart for their maintenance. They would then see, that they might as well attempt to turn the sun from its course, as to extract from their employers the same wages as at present, and to give a third less of their labour in return. Could they be taught something of the

nature and constitution of society, they would see
that those, who are above them in station, whom
they not unfrequently imagine to be their enemies,
would be inattentive to their own interests, did they
wish for aught but the prosperity and advancement
of the labouring population. They would not
be deceived by the ridiculously false assertion,
that two idlers exist and are supported for each
working man in the country, and they would understand and act upon the moral of the fable of
Menenius Agrippa, without the dreadful necessity
of it's practical enforcement. Would they turn
their attention to the inseparable connection between causes and effects, as well as to the actual
history of combinations, they might be persuaded
that strikes may lower but cannot raise wages, and
would perhaps shudder at the thought of being en-
tangled in the commission of the crimes we have
recounted, prompted as those crimes have been by
the very societies, to which they now look as opening the era of their regeneration.

SECTION II.

Effect of Combinations on the Introduction and Improvement of Machinery.

In nostros fabricata est machina muros.—VIRGIL. ÆN.

As hostility to machinery is a very prevalent
feeling among the working classes, it might be
supposed that they would turn all the power of
their Unions towards its suppression. In this at-

tempt, however, they have been singularly unsuccessful, and so far have they been from attaining,
or even approaching the attainment of this object,
that their efforts have led to an exactly contrary
result, and some of the most valuable and inge-
nious machines, that our manufactories can boast
of, actually owe their existence to the operation of
Trades' Unions.

The cotton trade affords one remarkable instance
of the truth of this observation. The evils inflicted
on this manufacture by strikes have been detailed ;
many years ago, the masters with the view of es-
caping these disastrous effects of the tyranny of
the Spinners' Union, requested the machine-
makers to attempt the construction of a self-acting
mule, that is, of a mule, which should perform its
work without the assistance of a spinner. For a
long time the attempt was regarded as hopeless,
difficulties stood in the way, which it is not easy
to describe, requiring, however, all the resources of
mechanical genius to surmount. But the successive efforts of mechanists have by degrees overcome
every obstacle, and the skill of Mr. Roberts,
an eminent machine-maker at Manchester, has
brought the invention to perfection. The most
extraordinary power of this machine, consists in
its manner of regulating the motion of the spindles,
when the mule is receding to its frame; during
this retrograde course, which carries the mule over
the space of $4\frac{1}{4}$ feet, about three times a minute,
the velocity of the spindles is constantly changing,

and this continues as many hours as they are filling with thread ; they exhibit, to speak mathe matically, a *fluxion* of movement ; during no two successive portions of time, however small, is the speed the same. The machine may now be seen in action in several mills, and almost appears to realize the finest results, that could be expected from human ingenuity.

The following evidence taken by the Committee of Manufactures and Commerce, which sat last Session, will shew the way in which the combination of the spinners is forcing the adoption of this machine. It is given by Mr. Graham, a Scotch manufacturer.

We are paying much higher in Glasgow, than they are paying in England for spinning the same numbers, and in consequence of this, we have been driven to employ machines, which may supersede those men (spinners).

Are you aware of any cotton spinning work, where the proprietors are turning out the old machinery in consequence of the combination of the workmen, and introducing self-acting mules ?—We are doing it ourselves.

Have you adopted the self-acting mule to get rid of combinations ? —Before adopting the self-acting mule, I had the plans drawn, and I called a deputation from the men in, and explained it to them, and I said, " You drive us either to take machines, or you drive us to bankruptcy, or to stop our works; here is an order going off to Manchester for self-acting mules ; we do not wish to introduce them, and we will be the last house to introduce them, if you will take the same wages that they have in Lancashire," and they said, " It is of no use, we are determined not to reduce our wages."

The introduction of this invention will eventually give a death blow to the Spinners' Union,

the members of which will have to thank themselves alone, for the creation of this destined agent
of their extinction. It is now rapidly coming into
use ; other advantages, besides the great one of
escape from the dictation of the workmen, are
found to attend it ; and in a few years the very
name of working spinner, as well as the follies and
oppression of their combination, will only be found
in history.

The turn-out of the Lancashire workmen in the
building trade, which has been mentioned in a
preceding page, has introduced a curious application of the steam-engine. This machine is now
employed in some towns, instead of manual labour,
in hoisting the various building materials to the
top of the edifice, where they are intended to be
used. The magnificent design of the Liverpool
custom-house is at the present moment rising into
existence by the assistance of steam. The following letter from a master-builder, who was one of
the principal sufferers in this strike, graphically
describes the circumstances attending the introduction of the improvement.

Liverpool, Feb. 7th, 1834.

Sir,

I have much pleasure in complying with your request, and
shall feel happy if any information, which I can afford, will be useful
to your purpose. About two years ago, the bricklayers' labourers,
whom I had at work at the new Custom House here, began to exhibit symptoms of rebellion, the building being unusually large, and
requiring much work. I found that, just in proportion as we were
hurried, the labourers began to relax and grow careless, and some-

times did not do a sufficient quantity of work to cover their own wages. My wits were accordingly set to work to discover a remedy. I well knew that if I resorted to severe measures, a general strike would have been the consequence, but as we had on the ground, about thirty-five yards from the front of the edifice, a seven horse steam-engine for the purpose of mixing up our lime and sand into mortar and making grout, I had the shaft of the mill lengthened, and a drum fixed upon it ; attached to this was a chain governed by a break, which we carried in a hollow trough under ground, and connected with a cross-beam placed upon two uprights on the top of the building. We then placed 300 bricks in a square box, slung it, and tried our engine. The bricks went up in fine style, and were received at the top by waggons placed on a light rail-way, furnished with cross slides, and the result was that two labourers could fill the boxes with bricks below, sling them on the chain, and two more receive them at the top, who, by the help of the rail-way conveyed them (weighing 23 cwt) to any part of the building with ease. We thus rendered useless the services of about twenty hod-carriers at once, at the cost of about 100*l.* in machinery. The remainder of the men were for a long period quiet, and would have continued so, had not the Trades' Unions virtually compelled them to strike, many of them against their wills. The contrivance just mentioned has acted so well, that, when in full work, we usually send to the top of the building 16,000 bricks per diem, with seven or eight tons of mortar and grout, the engine all the while doing its other accustomed work. This would only pay in large buildings ; in small erections, the expense of fixing the machinery would be too great ; but small high-pressure steam-engines are now made, which stand upon three feet square, consume about one cwt of coal a-day, and will hoist with sufficient rapidity 25 cwt. to any height, they are also sufficiently portable to be moved about in small carts ; or I am satisfied that a horse with a rope and pulley working through a snatch-block would be cheaper and better than the old system of manual labour.

The contractor for the stone-work at the new Custom House raises all his materials by a small engine, I think it is eight horse power, which cost him 150*l.*, and his other additional machinery about 200*l.* more. He sends his stones (varying from one to eleven tons in weight) up to the summit with perfect ease. His engine like ours is stationary, and his ropes run round the building to that part where the work is proceeding, and though they are sometimes 500 feet in length, no difficulty is experienced from this cause. We send up indiscriminately, bricks, stone, iron or timber ; the engine is much more tractable and civil than the hod-men, easier managed, keeps good hours, drinks no whiskey, and is never tired. I need hardly add that in a large building it is much cheaper, more expeditious and satisfactory than carrying up materials on men's shoulders. The time consumed by the men in *descending*, and by the slowness of their ascent consequent on the loss of strength caused by having to overcome the gravity of their own bodies, before they have strength to spare for carrying a heavy burden, makes the hod-carriers far inferior to the steam engine, more especially if we consider the constancy with which the latter works. I do not now fear a turn-out of hod-carriers, because I have proved that we can do very well without them, and I think that I now see many other modes of saving labour, which I should instantly avail myself of, were another strike to happen amongst my workmen. It is also obvious to myself that many of the uses to which machinery is now applied, may be traced to turn-outs, which, having subjected masters to inconveniences, have compelled them to scheme mechanical contrivances, that otherwise would not have been thought of. Feeling that improvements in mechanism will not eventually injure the labourer, yet I would not hastily adopt such, as would suddenly deprive a number of men of their subsistence, did not their own folly compel me to it. I am now quite sure that another strike or two will annihilate many hod-carriers and brickmakers, and this principle of hoisting by stationary or moveable steam-engines, will no doubt be adopted for many other purposes, if the operatives in particular departments endeavour to force their employers to pay a higher rate of wages than they can afford. For instance, we know that two stationary engines at each dock, with shafts and drums running along the quays, would discharge the cargoes of all the ships, with a tenth of the porters now employed ; at present I should be sorry to see it adopted, but I know before long it must be done.

I am, Sir, your very faithful Servant,

SAMUEL HOLME.

The machine lately introduced in the wool-combing business, has also been alluded to ; the history of its invention gives, in a short compass, a view of the process by which results of this kind are brought about. The Woolcombers' Union has been celebrated above a century, and several Acts of Parliament have been passed with the object of suppressing the power which it had acquired, and exercised with the usual bad consequences. Hence, many endeavours have been made to comb wool entirely by machinery, but with very partial success, till last year, when the whole of the combers in a large factory struck, upon which the proprietors turned their attention to this machine, applied their skill and capital to its improvement, and in a short time brought it to such perfection, as completely to supersede the employment of woolcombers.* It consists of two large wheels, set with spikes, and which are made to approach and recede alternately from each other ; the spokes, fellies, and axles are all hollow, by means of which steam is kept constantly flowing through every

---

* Till within a few years of the time when this machine was introduced, it could not have been made, though it might have been imagined, and every part and principle necessary to its construction clearly and accurately described. The reason is, that the skill and nicety of execution necessary to the manufacturing of such a machine, or of any machine requiring delicate adjustments, did not exist. The principle of Bramah's press was known two centuries before its application, but was a barren truth, till mechanism had advanced sufficiently to give it an existence.— See *Babbage on the Decline of Science.*

part of the machine, like the arteries in the human body, diffusing the required warmth to every corner of the engine. This invention is now daily coming into wider use; it performs its work both better and cheaper than by the old process, and before no long period has elapsed, the trade of wool-comber, like that of cotton-spinner, will cease to exist.

Mr. Babbage, in his " Economy of Manufactures," has given two other instances of invention of modes for superseding human labour, owing to strikes among workmen; one occurred in the manufacture of gun-barrels, and the other in that of iron tubes in general; and, doubtless, many other cases might be found, in which a similar process had taken place.

The obvious result of this forced and premature adoption of new machinery, is to displace labour with inconvenient rapidity; and, instead of improvement proceeding by those gently varying gradations, which characterise its natural progress, it advances, as it were, *per saltum*, and comes upon the workman unprepared for the change, which his course of life must subsequently undergo. The counter effect in retarding the improvement of machinery, sometimes caused by combinations, is so trivial, as hardly to deserve mention. But whatever power they may have in this way, the end of it must be to increase still further the evil just alluded to, and to make the progress in the application of substitutes for labour, more fluctuating and irregular. At one time they are unnaturally held back, at another pushed forward.

It would be a glaring absurdity to suppose that the improvement of machinery can be really hurtful to society, or lessen the demand for labour in the country which employs it, when we have the example of Manchester before us, where, within a radius of forty miles, more human beings are collected together, and substitutes for labour more extensively used, than on any other spot on earth, and where, in addition, wages are for the most part enormously high. It undoubtedly is productive of transient injury by the displacement, which it causes of manual labour in those operations to which it is applied. But this evil is trivial if the displacement be slow, and is formidable only when it is pushed on, as in the cases above-mentioned, with sudden violence.

We might view these inventions with unmixed pleasure, on account of their use to society, and even—considering the force of example—without much regret for the retribution they inflict on the offenders, were it possible to put out of sight some of the evils which may for a season follow their introduction. The community certainly gains by such mechanical improvements, which, since they spring from hostility to combinations, may be considered an indirect effect of them, and form, as far as we are aware, the only benefits those bodies have bestowed upon their country, in return for the violence and oppressions of which they have been guilty.

SECTION III.

Proposed alterations in the Laws respecting Combinations.

What then is liberty ? —Liberty, I would answer, so far as it is possible for it to exist in a society of beings, whose interests are almost perpetually opposed to each other, consists in this—that every man, while he respects the persons of others, and allows them quietly to enjoy the produce of their own industry, be certain himself likewise to enjoy the produce of his own industry, and that his person be also secure.—*De Lolme.*

IT may be supposed that a remedy to the numerous evils that have been described, would be found in a re-enactment of the Combination Laws. To a proposal of this nature we should give a decided and unqualified opposition. Such laws would be both ineffectual and unjust, and either reason ought to be sufficient for their condemnation. The experience of centuries has shewn, that legal impediments to combinations have no power in suppressing them, and that their only effect is to render the members more ferocious and secret in their operations. Every trade in Dublin was united in the closest bonds of union, long before the repeal of the Combination Laws, and both there and elsewhere outrages have been, upon the whole, less frequent since the abolition of those enactments. Of more than 100 witnesses examined before the Combination Committee of 1824, only one wished their continuance, and even he, to a certain extent, bore testimony with the rest to their inefficiency;

the evidence taken by the Committee, which sat
in the succeeding year, was equally decided on
this point ; it would, therefore, be absurd to resort
to an expedient thus universally condemned. Combinations seem to have been more systematically
conducted and more extensive since the alteration
of the law respecting them, but they have also
been more open and direct ; the extent and character of the danger cannot now be misunderstood,
nor a remedy applied in ignorance.

The first and simplest form in which Combinations present themselves, is that of meetings of
workmen called together on particular emergen-
cies, for the purpose of considering whether the
rate of wages given, or proposed to be given, by
the masters is sufficiently high; and also of passing
resolutions declaratory of their opinion on the subject, leaving it to each individual workman, whether or not a party to the meeting, to behave as he
may think fit upon such resolutions. Occasional
unions of this sort, whose only object is to do that
in common, which beyond all question, might be
done by each member severally, and supplied with
no other means of procuring combined action, than
the conviction, which may arise from their discussions, and the shame which will attach to the apparent desertion of the common cause, are undoubtedly entitled, if not to the favour, at any rate
to the sufferance of the law.

The next shape in which Combinations are to be
considered, is that of permanent clubs or con-

federacies, calculated by their very permanence to facilitate on each occasion, as it may occur, the union of the workmen against the masters, and possessed of funds from which they may supply those, who, in pursuance of a common resolution, may refuse to work at the rate of wages offered, the means of subsisting without work. As these are nothing more than contrivances enabling the members of such Societies to do certain lawful acts with less prejudice to themselves, and with more efficacy in regard to the object sought, without any compulsion being attempted upon those who refuse to concur in such acts, it would require very strong grounds of public expediency to impeach the right of the workmen to form even such permanent and systematic Unions. But in all such confederacies it should be observed, there is a law enabling the Society to expel any member who should refuse to abide by any resolution on the subject of wages, adopted by the majority, and such member would at the same time be deprived of all benefit from the sums previously contributed by him in the way of subscription. Such a forfeiture is undoubtedly a compulsory process, and it is a forfeiture exacted for the doing a lawful act, that is to say, for working at such wages as a man may be able to obtain. Whether such rule should be suffered to exist, or at any rate to be acted upon, is a matter of some little doubt, though the better opinion seems to be against legislative interference. Such a condition of forfeiture as that just described, may be one,

which, from considerations of public policy, the
law perhaps would not enforce, but relieve from,
when enforced ; but that affords no sufficient reason for visiting it with a penalty, nor is it agree-
able to the tenor of the law in other matters, to
treat agreements as criminal, merely because they
are null. So long then as Combinations confine
themselves within the limits above described, they
may be properly and safely left free from any further control than such as the common principles
and practice of our laws will supply.

But the case becomes wholly different, when
those who combine to refuse work, are not simply
passive in their proceedings, but endeavour, by
violence and intimidation, to induce others to follow their example. At this point the law ought to
interfere, and in order to see the mode in which
that interference should be exercised, it will be
necessary to detail the way, in which the evil that
it is intended to remedy, is felt and inflicted.

When a strike has taken place in any factory,
men are always stationed to keep watch on the
building, and also on every avenue leading to it,
whose business it is to prevent fresh workmen being
engaged in the place of those who have turned out.
Every labouring man who appears to be seeking
employment in the direction of the factory, or, having accepted employment in it, is returning from
it, is stopt and interrogated, and should he prove
refractory, is threatened or maltreated. This system of *picqueting* mills has been carried to the

greatest extent in Manchester, where the obnoxious factory is always watched by five or six men, unknown in the immediate neighbourhood, and who, on a given signal, can be reinforced to the extent of three hundred. These picquets are regularly relieved, by night and by day, with as much order and method as is observed by an army in a hostile country; and so effectual are they in producing the desired end, that an establishment is not unfrequently kept in a state of literal siege; no one can enter or leave it without danger of molestation; and if fresh workmen have by any means been introduced, beds and provisions are prepared for them within the walls of the factory.

It is absolutely necessary for the protection of liberty, that some legal means should exist for removing these picquets. Any person connected with the establishment so watched, or police-officer at the request of such person, might be authorized to apprehend, without warrants, any of these picquets, and take them before a magistrate, who should have the power of summarily convicting them in a penalty or three months imprisonment. In no part of the proceedings should it be necessary to have the names of the offenders, as they are rarely known to those in the neighbourhood, being always purposely sent for from a distance. To those who may object to the tyrannous and oppressive character of such an enactment, we should remark, that nothing can exceed the tyranny of the practices it is intended to put down. A whole neighbourhood is kept in awe by a system of intimidation, of which these picquets are the primary agents. It is not likely that an innocent person could ever suffer from such a law; there is no difficulty in pointing out without danger of mistake, the five or six persons, who may be watching a factory for several hours at a time, nor is it probable that any one would act in this way for the sake of harmless amusement.

The next end, which imperiously requires a new act, is the more effectual punishment of outrages committed in pursuance of the objects of a Combination. The Committee which sat in 1824, and by whose recommendation the Combination Laws were repealed, seem to have been fully aware of the importance of this object. One of their resolutions states, "That it is absolutely necessary, when repealing the Combination Laws, to enact such a law as may efficiently and by summary process, punish either workmen or masters, who by threats, intimidation, or acts of violence, should interfere with that perfect freedom, which ought to be allowed to each party, of employing his labour or capital in the manner he may deem most advantageous." To the neglect of this advice, many of the evils now complained of may be attributed. The law of 1824, which removed all impediments to combination, gave two magistrates the power of punishing, on the testimony of two witnesses, by two months imprisonment and hard labour, any one convicted of an assault committed to forward the purposes of a Union, and no appeal to the Sessions was allowed. This was found inefficient, and the Committee, which sat in the ensuing year, reiterated the recommendation of the former one, declaring that to the prevention of outrages against those refusing to join Unions, they attached " the highest importance, as being indispensably necessary, not less to the real interest of the working classes, than to the public peace."

In consequence, a fresh act was passed, by which three months imprisonment was made the punishment instead of two, and one witness only was required to prove the offence. These were doubtless beneficial alterations, but unfortunately the benefit was more than marred, by introducing a clause giving the right of appeal to the Sessions. This was in direct contradiction to the advice of the Committee, and the result has been, that the cases are almost always decided on at the Sessions, and in the intermediate time between the committal and the trial, either some flaw is found in the indictment, or the witnesses are intimidated, and the prisoner escapes. And thus, what ought to be the chief object in all criminal enactments,—to make the punishment follow the offence with speed and certainty, is wholly neglected.

There is one other point in which Combinations as they now exist, are proper objects of penal legislation, that is to say, in respect of the oaths administered upon admission to the members of such Societies. Voluntary oaths, that is, all such oaths as are not exacted by some legal authority should be, in every case, if not actually prohibited, at any rate discouraged, affording as they do without any adequate object, increased opportunities to the great moral crime of perjury, and that too in cases, where the offence is likely to be further multiplied by impunity; the law not interfering to punish the breach or falsity of such oaths, as the law does not itself impose. But the objection to voluntary oaths acquires much greater weight, when they are not only voluntary but secret, and used as a bond of union by large bodies of men, deriving perhaps an additional force, as we have seen they do in the cases before us, from the cunningly devised terrors of a superstitious ritual. But on this head it seems no new enactments are required. The law, as it now stands, if the construction put upon it by the highest authority be correct, is amply sufficient; every member of a Trades' Union, who shall bind himself to obey the decision of the majority, though that obedience be restricted to a mere refusal to work, and not to disclose the transactions of the Society, being guilty of felony, and liable to be transported for seven years. The generality of workmen would doubtless be surprised if they heard this; yet such is the effect of the language held by the judges of the King's Bench, particularly Lord Chief Justice Ellenborough, in the case of "Rex v. Marks," reported in the third volume of East. They considered that an association, which had not for its object to stir up mutiny or sedition, but merely aimed at raising the rate of wages, or regulating the concerns of a particular trade, though it did not fall within the preamble of the act (37 Geo. III. c. 123.) was subject to its provisions and penalties, in respect of any oaths of obedience or concealment required from the parties to such association. This, it is true, is only the expression of a judicial opinion, the case not calling for a decision on the point in question, and perhaps some difficulty might arise now in obtaining in a similar case a conviction under the act referred to. If, however, there be any reasonable doubt of the efficacy of that statute, and there does seem great reason to doubt whether cases of this sort were intended to be embraced by it, the deficiency should be supplied by the legislature. But if that, in the opinion of competent judges, should not be deemed necessary, then no other alterations in the law are required, than increasing the facilities for suppressing acts of intimidation. Could this object be effectually attained, an important step would be taken towards putting an end to Trades' Unions altogether, and many of them must instantly dissolve, holding their existence, as they may be said to do, on the tenure of intimidation. Mr. Campbell, the sheriff-substitute for Renfrewshire, says in his evidence before a Parliamentary Committee, " Their mode of effecting their objects was chiefly by means of intimidation, and without that I do not see that the combination could hang together many weeks ; for when a struggle takes place between the cotton-spinners and their masters, it is necessary to the success of the workmen, that they should all join together, and therefore it is quite indispensable for them, as experience has shewn with us at least, to control their fellow-workmen, so as to procure that unanimity by any means. Those who do not go into their measures are termed ' knobs, and it is quite an understood thing, that these knobs are to be persecuted in various ways, and if necessary, their lives are to be attempted." Mr. Robinson, the sheriff-depute of Lanarkshire, also speaks to the same purport. He says, " I think the effect of the acts of intimidation, taken generally, has been to bind together, and to create and give effect to the existing co-operation among these combinations. I think that without intimidation, they would individually and collectively more speedily fall to pieces, because it is through the medium of intimidation, that they, in a great measure, collect or obtain the funds, which they distribute in furtherance of their purposes."

The public voice could hardly condemn the severity of the enactments, that have been proposed, were the monstrous tyranny they are intended to counteract fully made known. Nor could the workmen themselves object to them with any degree of propriety or consistency, since both in conversation and in the documents they publish, they invariably express their disapproval of acts of intimidation, declaring that they are contrary to their rules, and that it is their earnest desire to leave to every one the free disposal of his labour.

Those whose lives and properties have been endangered by these illegal associations, have a right to call on Government to employ some additional means for their suppression. Those who wish for the prosperity of our trade, and what is of far more importance, the prosperity and happiness of the working classes, should equally desire their extinction. Those who hate oppression, should give their suffrages for the putting down of these most capricious and irresponsible of despotisms. They are alike hurtful to the workmen, who form them; to the capitalists, who are the objects of their hostility; and to the public in general, who more remotely feel their effects. Were we asked to give a definition of a Trades' Union, we should say that it was a Society whose constitution is the worst of democracies—whose power is based on outrage—whose practice is tyranny—and whose end is self-destruction.*

---

* For a more extended account of the past and present state of the Law relating to Combinations, see a well-written article in the last January number of the Law Magazine.

APPENDIX.

RULES.

I.

That this Society be denominated the "National Friendly Society" of operative Worsted Manufacturers, and other industriousoperatives.

II.

That the objects of this Society shall be the moral and intellectual improvement of it's members, and an equalization and advance of wages, when considered proper and practicable in the trades connected with this institutiou.

III.

That each trade admitted into this Society shall keep its own money, but shall pledge themselves to advance such sums of money as may be required to assist any other trade belonging to the same, which may come in collision with their employers. Each trade that may have advanced such money, to be assisted in the same manner when the necessity of the case may require such assistance.

IV.

That a Grand Master, Deputy Grand Master, and Grand Secretary, be the governing officers of this Society, to be chosen at the Grand Lodge Meeting out of the delegates then present, whose duty it shall be to transact the general business of the Society, to visit the different

Lodges, to arrange and appoint the opening of new one's, and to revise, methodise and prepare all matters connected with this Society, rules excepted; the Deputy Grand Master to act in the absence of the Grand Master, but both shall not be paid for sitting at one time.

v.

That the Grand Lodge be constituted of representatives from every district to be sent as follows :—for every district containing 4 Lodges and under, one delegate ; and 8 and under, 2 delegates ; 12 and under, 3 delegates ; and so on in proportion, to meet on the 1st Monday in February, and the 1st Monday in August.

vi.

That any Lodge that is not satisfied with the above rule, shall have the privilege of sending a delegate to the Grand Lodge Meeting, exclusive of the funds of the Society, and that any district, having a separate trade formed into one Lodge shall have the privilege to send a delegate, that there may be a representation of each trade in such district at the Grand Lodge Meeting ; and that each delegate shall be allowed to vote according to the number of Lodges he may represent.

vii.

That this Society be formed into districts or divisions, as the extension of the Society may require ; and that a district delegate meeting be held every three months, to examine the accompt of the district and appoint the district Grand Officers and Committee, who shall transact the business for the time being, and every district shall have the power to arrange this Committee as they think proper.

viii.

That a Grand Committee or council of direction be formed, to consist of seven delegates, one from each trade in the adjoining districts, to be chosen every Grand Lodge Meeting, the district to have the power to change the person when they think proper, five of the Committee shall form a quorum, and this Committee alone shall decide upon the nature of strikes, except in cases of reduction, which the district authorities may decide upon, if necessity require it. The expulsion of Lodges and the general business of the Society may be brought under their notice.

IX.

That the Grand Head shall remove annually to the following places, viz.—Leeds, Bradford, Keighley and Halifax.

X.

That there shall be a monthly report drawn up by every Lodge in each district, and sent to the corresponding Society of the district, of all receipts and disbursements, who paid to, and what for, also the number of members in each Lodge. Such report to be made by the Secretaries of the districts to the Grand Secretary, and that he transmit such reports monthly to the various districts.

XI.

That every member engaged in a legal strike shall receive the weekly allowance of 7s. and every one, who has a family shall receive 1s. for each child, under ten years of age, that is unemployed, and 1s. for his wife, and shall be exempt from paying his levies, and every half member shall receive his pay in the same proportion.

XII.

That any Member being supported from this Society and discovered at work, if he neglect to inform the committee or officers, he shall be called before the district committee for his conduct, and must abide by their decision.

XIII.

That if any member have an accusation to prefer against any other member, he shall prefer it through the medium of the resident to the Committee of the Grand Lodge, to which such member belongs. The Committee shall try the accused party, and if found guilty, but still finds himself dissatisfied, he shall bring his case before the District Committee, whose decision shall be final.

XIV.

That every Lodge, on being legally applied to for the money they may have in hand, by the proper authorities, shall pay it on demand, or remit it within three days after the meeting of the said Lodge. Any Lodge refusing to comply with this regulation, shall be subject to a fine of one pound, which if they refuse to pay, the case shall be brought before the District Committee. If the said Lodge be still dissatisfied, the case shall be referred to the Council of Direction, the decision of which shall be final.

XV.

That if any member or Lodge have any just ground of complaint against either of the Grand Officers, he or they shall make the charge in writing to the Chairman of the District Committee, where the Grand Lodge is held, when the case shall undergo proper examination, after which, if the officer or officers be found guilty, he or they shall be suspended, and a just report of the examination be handed over to the Committee of direction, whose decision of the case shall be final. Any member preferring fruitless or vexatious charges against the Grand Officers shall be fined 5s.

XVI.

That all children under fourteen years of age shall pay 1 d. per week, as levies, and receive, when on strike, 3s.

K

per week; all females, from fourteen to seventeen years of age, shall pay 1½d. per week, and when on strike, receive 4s. 6d. per week; all above that age shall pay 2d. per week, and when on strike, receive 6s. per week; the males from fourteen to sixteen years of age, shall pay 1½d. per week, and receive, when on strike, 4s. 6d. per week; those from sixteen to eighteen, shall pay 2d. per week, and when on strike, receive 6s. per week; at which age they are allowed to be admitted as full members of this Society.

XVII.

That no individuals, having the power to command the labour of any individual or individuals, his own family excepted, shall be admitted as a member of this Society.

XVIII.

That the officers of every Lodge shall, at the expiration of every three months, vacate their situations, when those of them that are not re-elected, shall have their places filled by other members.

XIX.

That if any member of this Society shall disclose any of its secret transactions to a stranger, he shall be expelled this Society, never more to be admitted.

XX.

That should any member of this Society be known to boast of his earnings or superior abilities as to the quantity or quality of work he can do, he shall be fined 1s. 6d. and be suspended the Society until such fine be paid.

XXI.

That should any member of this Society be deprived of his employment through opposing a reduction of wages, and another be known to take his place or situation, he shall be for ever expelled from this Society.

XXII.

That no member shall be allowed to enter any Lodge, or obtain any relief when on strike, who is more than six months in arrears, unless he intends to pay up his levies that night, except he can show a satisfactory reason for not paying up such arrears.

XXIII.

That should any member be reduced by sickness, or otherwise, so as to be unable to pay his levies, he shall make his case known to the Committee of his own Lodge, that such lenity may be shown him, as the case may require.

XXIV.

That should any member violate any of the rules of this Society, and another have a knowledge thereof, and neglect to inform the officers of the Lodge to which the said member belongs, he shall be fined 1s. for such neglect.

XXV.

That as soon as any member enters the Lodge, and has given the inward sign, the Wardens shall order such member to attend the Secretary, if he intends to pay any levies that evening, and the Secretary shall not receive any monies after 9 o'clock at night, unless through a press of business, the officers of the Lodge think it expedient to take money afterwards.

XXVI.

That should the outside Tiler knowingly admit any member in a state of intoxication, he shall be fined 6d. for every such offence.

XXVII.

That every person entering this Society, shall pay the sum of 1s. as entrance money, towards defraying the expenses incurred by the Lodge, and he shall afterwards pay 3*d*. per week, or more, when the authorities deem it necessary for the protection of trade, to go to the use of the Society, and support of the trade at large.

XXVIII.

That should any person be proposed to become a member of this Society, and any member object to the member so proposed, if any disclose the name of the objector, he shall be fined 2*s*. whether the person objected to be admitted or not.

XXIX.

That the Secretary of each Lodge shall read the minute of the evening every Lodge night before the Lodge is closed. The word Brother shall be used only during Lodge hours.

XXX.

That any member who may be injured by his employers or otherwise, shall state his complaint to the President of his Lodge, who will then call upon him, and he rising from his seat, shall address the Lodge ; any brother contradicting him, or saying, " you should have joined the Union sooner," shall be fined 6*d*.

XXXI.

That every member of this Society shall attend his own Lodge, to receive the new signs and pass words, the same to be changed every Grand Lodge meeting, or oftener if required, and that the Grand Secretary shall acquaint every district when so changed.

XXXII.

That all applications for new Lodges must be made to the district Grand Master, or Grand Secretary, six at least must be made beforehand, and they must have the making money of nine others at the opening of the Lodge, those fifteen to be the founders of the Lodge.

XXXIII.

That no hearing shall be given to discussions of visiting brothers until the regular business of the Lodge be closed, unless permitted by the President, and the majority of the members present.

XXXIV.

That if any delegate do not attend the Grand Lodge Meeting at the time appointed, he shall be fined 1s. and for neglecting after the conclusion of the Grand Lodge business to attend the Lodge he may represent (if required), he shall be fined 10s. except he can show a satisfactory reason for his non-attendance at such Lodges.

XXXV.

That if any member of our Society allow any black sheep to lodge or work in their houses, they shall be considered equally culpable ; or any person not entitled to enter his own Lodge, except his own wife, children, brothers, or sisters, shall also be considered equally guilty, or if he should associate with either of the above description of persons after a remonstrance from his own Lodge, he shall be expelled this Society.

XXXVI.

That no member shall be allowed to draw his clearance or transfer from his Lodge, after a fine be laid, until the said fine be paid.

XXXVII.

That no member of this Society shall undertake to learn any individual the art of wool-combing, weaving, or sorting, if above the age of fourteen years.

XXXVIII.

That each Grand Lodge delegate in the Bradford district, receive 3s. 6d. per day in addition to their dinner, and that every delegate from the three adjacent districts, viz. Leeds, Keighley, and Halifax, shall receive 5s. per day in addition to their dinner. That those who come a greater distance be allowed mileage, according to their distance; those under 100 miles 2d., those under 200 miles 3d., and those above 200 miles 4d. per mile.

XXXIX.

It is recommended that each member shall belong to the nearest Lodge to his own residence, in order to organize the Society, and prevent members from being so much in arrears in the books as heretofore, except they give a satisfactory reason for remaining at distant Lodges.

XL.

That all dispensations for the future shall be signed and sealed in a legal manner, and that all dispensations having no seal attached to them be brought by the district delegate, within one month of this date, to get a legal signature, and also a legal seal.

XLI.

That Quakers shall be admitted into this Society, by his or their affirmation, the same as in a Court of Justice.

XLII.

That the inward sign be given to the Wardens, instead of the outside password, at the opening of Lodges.

XLIII.

That no ale be allowed to any officers in our Lodges except the outside Tiler.

XLIV.

That each Lodge shall have the power to make their own bye-laws, if not in opposition to the general rules of this Society.

XLV.

That each Corresponding Secretary shall personally produce his books, for inspection, at the Grand Lodge meetings, to stand against the Grand Secretary's report.

XLVI.

That after an application has been made to, and granted by, the grand district Officers to open a Lodge, the nearest Lodge shall be appointed to open the same, with a remuneration of 6*d.*, and 2*d.* per mile.

XLVII.

Should any member of this Society be found embezzling any money or other property belonging to this Society, he or they shall be suspended until such money be paid back, or the property made good, and satisfaction given to the district officers.

XLVIII.

No member shall be allowed to go to any place with an intent to get employment, where an advance of wages has been gained, or any difference taken place betwixt the master and men, relative to our Society, for the limited time of two months : but should the employer think proper to employ more hands, they shall be sent, on due authority, from the nearest Committee.

XLIX.

That the wages of the Grand Officers in future be paid out of the district where the Grand Lodge is held.

The following are the Rules of one of the Lodges that compose the preceding Association.

I.

That this Society be called the Friendly Society of Operative Worsted or Stuff Manufacturers.

II.

That the objects of this Society shall be to advance and equalize the price of labour in every branch of the trades which we receive into this Society.

III.

That if any member of this Society shall disclose any of its transactions to a stranger, or strangers, he shall be expelled the Society, never more to be admitted.

IV.

That should any member of this Society be known to boast of his superior ability as to either the quantity or quality of work he can do, either in public or private company, he shall pay a fine of 2s. 6d., or be expelled this Society.

V.

That should any member of this Society be thrown out of employment through seeking an advance or opposing a reduction of his wages, and another be known to take his place or situation, he shall be suspended twelve months, but if at the expiration of his suspension, he come forward and acknowledge his fault, and manifest a desire to become a member, he shall again become a regular member by paying up his contributions in full.

VI.

That no member shall be admitted into any Lodge, or be entitled to any benefit whatever, that is more than 3s. in arrears, unless he intend to pay his contributions that night; and any member who neglects paying his subscriptions till they amount to 2s. 6d. shall be excluded, unless he can show a satisfactory reason for not paying up his arrears.

VII.

That should any member be reduced, by sickness or otherwise, so as to be unable to pay his contributions, he shall make his case known to the Committee, and such lenity will be shown him as the case may seem to require.

VIII.

That if any member violates any of the rules of this Society, and another member have a knowledge of it, and neglect to inform the officers of the Lodge to which he belongs, he shall be fined 1s. 6d. for such neglect.

IX.

That so soon as any member enters any Lodge, and gives the inward sign, he shall immediately attend the Secretary, if he intend to pay any contributions that night, and the Secretary shall not receive any subscription money after ten o'clock at night.

X.

That all the members serving on a turn-out shall be exempt from paying any contributions while they remain out, and when the strike shall be terminated, they will owe the same as at its commencement. Same privilege to members without work.

XI.

That should the outside Tiler admit any one to enter the Lodge in a state of intoxication, he shall be fined 6d.

XII.

That every person on entering this Society shall pay 1s. entrance-money, to go towards defraying the expenses of the Lodge, and he shall afterwards pay 2d. per fortnight, to go to the use of this Society, and support of the trade.

XIII.

That should any person be proposed to become a member of this Society, and a member raise any objection to the person so proposed, and another member disclose the name of the objector, he shall be fined 5s., whether the person objected to be admitted or not : should he refuse to pay it when called before a Committee, he shall be expelled the Society.

XIV.

That the Secretary shall give the minutes of the evening, every regular Lodge night, before the Lodge is closed.

XV.

That the word " brother," shall be used during Lodge hours only.

XVI.

That any member who may be injured by his Master or otherwise, shall state his complaint in writing to the President, and the President shall call upon him, and he rising from his seat shall address the Lodge ; any member contradicting him during the relation of his grievance, or saying to him, " you should have joined the Union sooner," shall be fined 1s.

XVII.

That every member who rises three times to speak on one subject shall be fined 1s.

Friendly Associated Coal Miner's Union Society,
established March, 1830.

Formed for the purpose of preventing wages being reduced, and for relieving such distressed workmen as are out of employment, owing to their employers reducing their wages, which are already so very low that it is almost impossible to obtain the necessaries of life, for themselves and families.

Every Lodge in this Society, shall be governed by a Committee chosen at a General Meeting of the Members of their respective Lodges ; and such Committee shall consist of seven in number, &c. &c. They shall choose and appoint a Secretary and Treasurer to serve for the space of one year, with a salary.

That there shall be four persons appointed by the Committee, to inspect or examine into any dispute, work, or account, that may happen to arise between any master and workman : and on receiving notice from any member of this Society, such inspectors are immediately to inquire into the disputes, and report the case to the Committee.

That if any difference should arise between master and workman, with respect to lowering the wages, the men so disagreeing with their employers, shall immediately inform one, or all of the inspectors, who shall examine into the dispute, and report the same to a Committee Meeting, which Committee shall consider of the justness of such reduction.

That if any members shall assault, or abuse any master or person employed, as foreman, or manager in the business of Coal Mining, or do wilful damage to their houses or property, or make any disturbance or riot against the public, &c. &c. he shall be expelled this Society ; as this Society is intended for the encouragement of honesty, sobriety, industry, and peaceable behaviour.

That if any member speak disrespectfully of the State and Laws of the Nation, His Majesty, or either of the Houses of Parliament, or any Magistrate, he shall forfeit 2s. 6d. for every such offence.

Quarterly meetings to be held of three persons out of each Committee of each Lodge in this Society, on the first Monday in January, April, July, and October.

2s. 6d. forfeit for coming to the club-room intoxicated ; or if any member game, encourage gaming, offer to lay a wager, challenge another to fight, use any language in order to lessen any member as to his knowledge, or understanding in his trade, or shall debate about politics, religion, quarrel, or cause any quarrelling, he shall pay a fine of 6*d.* for each offence, and make an apology to the chairman ; and if two brothers quarrel and fight, they shall pay a fine of 5*s.* jointly.

That there shall be a President and Vice President, appointed by, and out of the Committee of every Lodge, who shall act six months, and such Chairman shall strictly command order, and any person disobeying such order shall forfeit 3*d.*

The meeting to begin and end with a prayer composed for the occasion.

Had the writer of the foregoing pages availed himself of all the occurrences, which have marked the extravagance of Trades' Unions, during the passage of his work through the press, his notes would have been swollen beyond their just limits. Part of London is now (March 7th) in darkness from a strike amongst the workmen at the gas establishments. Scarcely a town in England has escaped the infliction of a turn-out, and were he to state that the working classes, have taxed themselves to the amount of one million during the past year, in these futile attempts to raise wages, the calculation would probably be below the truth.

THE END.

ERRATUM.

Page 36, line 7 from bottom, *for* Coals per pound, *read* Coals per 112 pounds.

NORMAN AND SKEEN, PRINTERS, 29, MAIDEN LANE.

British Labour Struggles:
Contemporary Pamphlets 1727-1850

An Arno Press/New York Times Collection

The Factory Act of 1833. 1833-1834.

Richard Oastler: King of Factory Children. 1835-1861.

The Battle for the Ten Hours Day Continues. 1837-1843.

The Factory Education Bill of 1843. 1843.

Prelude to Victory of the Ten Hours Movement. 1844.

Sunday Work. 1794-1856.

Demands for Early Closing Hours. 1843.

Conditions of Work and Living: The Reawakening of the English Conscience. 1838-1844.

Improving the Lot of the Chimney Sweeps. 1785-1840.

The Rising of the Agricultural Labourers. 1830-1831.

The Aftermath of the "Lost Labourers' Revolt". 1830-1831.